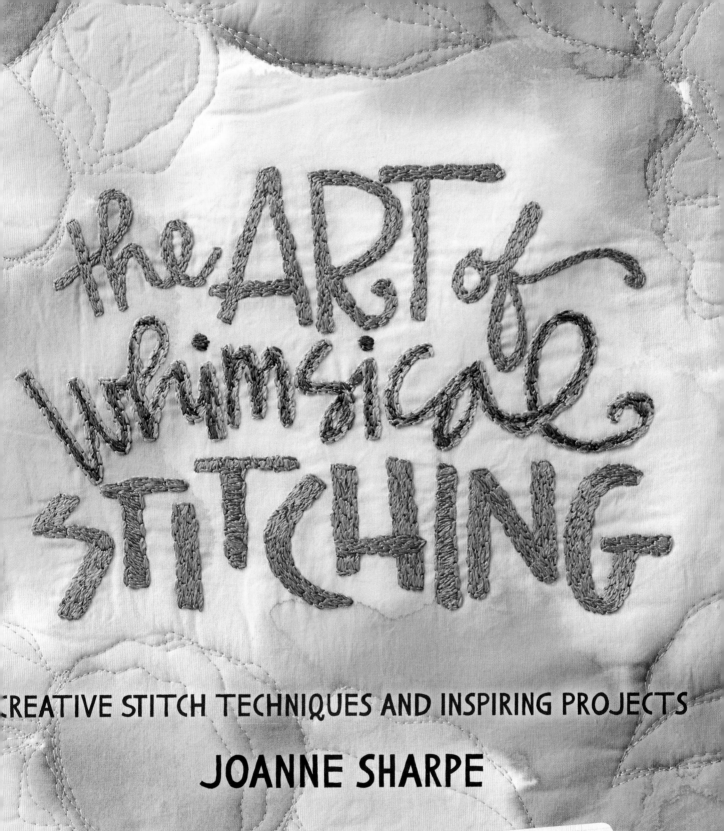

the ART of whimsical STITCHING

CREATIVE STITCH TECHNIQUES AND INSPIRING PROJECTS

JOANNE SHARPE

INTERWEAVE.
interweave.com

» See page 48 to learn the Coloring Blocks technique.

CONTENTS

4   Introduction: Just Sew for It!

Part 1: MIXED-MEDIA STITCHING BASICS

10   The Art of the Stitch
14   The Art Sewing Studio
15   Build Your Fabric Stash
18   A Fabric Coloring and Painting Palette
23   Thread-cetera
26   Artful Supplies and Tools
30   Stitching Must-Haves
34   Choosing Color Stories

Part 2: WHIMSICAL TECHNIQUES AND FUNK-TIONAL PROJECTS

40   Paint to Stitch
44   *Bursting Blooms Tote Bag*

48   Coloring Blocks
52   *Flower Pop Sculpted Pillow*

56   Decorative Machine Doodles
58   *Fancy Quilted Pouch*

62   Doodle Handstitching
64   *Doodle Stitch Journal*

68   Stencil and Sew
70   *Pen and Brush Tied Roll*

74   Artful Alphabets Appliqué
78   *Whimsical Words Art Quilt*

82   Sketch and Stitch
84   *Alphabet Baby Quilt*

88   Artfully Embellished Embroidery
90   *Crazy Patch Table Runner*

94   Mixed-Media Art Fabric
96   *Travel Memories Story Quilt*

100 Fabric Stash Collage
104 *Butterflies Book Cover*

108 Scrappy Snips Collage Cloth
110 *Patchwork Peeper Keeper*

114 Whimsical Wools
116 *Wonderfully Woolly Needle Book*

Part 3: THE ARTFUL IMAGERY SKETCHBOOK

122 Imagery Transfer Tips
123 Doodle Blooms
124 Winged Things
125 Hearts, Houses, Teatime

126 Doodle Shapes, Starry Night,
     Swirls and Twirls
127 Whimsical Words
128 Templates

132 Quilting and Sewing Basics
138 Embroidery Stitches
142 Index
142 Acknowledgments
143 Resources

» *Joy.* 11" × 15" (28 × 38 cm); fused appliqué.
See page 74 for more examples of Artful
Alphabets Appliqué.

JUST SEW FOR IT!

The Art of Whimsical Stitching is a playful exploration of mixed-media art, sewing, quilting, embroidery, and the infinite possibilities of combining them. It's a collection of my personal pieces interwoven with inspirational ideas, techniques, and projects for you to try.

My first artistic love was lettering. In my book *The Art of Whimsical Lettering,* I shared my techniques for creating lettering styles using your own handwriting. Once I had ventured down the path of combining art and sewing, though, I became so excited, I knew I would end up sharing the experience with the art community. That was the driving force behind this, my second book. While not all of the practices in these pages are necessarily new, I have penned this guide for an artful journey that shows how to combine art and stitching into creative practice with minimum inhibition or intimidation, always encouraging you to stretch and find new ways to do familiar things.

Who will love this way of art?

This book is for mixed-media artists, general crafters, sewists, and adventurous quilters looking to flex their creative muscles and take off in new directions of personal expression. For visual artists, it's a resource to learn how to add sewing and quilting to your repertoire. For quilters and sewists, it's an opportunity to explore painting and drawing supplies and tactics that will take your fabric creations to the next level. It's all about permission to play, to venture outside the traditional sewing (or paint) box and make art in a new realm.

What's the big idea?

The Art of Whimsical Stitching is a "tasting menu," a sampler of sewing, stitching, and art ideas and techniques with a colorful, unconventional spin. This is the book I wished I had when I was researching how to transfer my mixed-media art skills into sewing, quilting, hand embroidery, and machine stitching. Subject-specific information seemed overwhelming or intimidating and yet at the same time too narrow—there was so much I wanted to explore in quilting, embroidery, and textile art. Even though I had acquired the basics of many of these crafts as a young girl, I was looking to explore new ways to elevate, enhance, and reinvent my art with stitching, fibers, and textiles. I knew I could transfer many of the supplies I already had in my mixed-media stash, but I wanted

» **Doodle Journal.** *5" × 7" (12.5 × 18 cm) (closed); dye color; hand embroidery. See more examples of Doodle Handstitching on page 62 and instructions for creating a similar custom journal on page 64.*

» **Create, Love, Inspire.** *12" × 9" (30.5 × 23 cm); needlefelting, hand embroidery. Learn more about Whimsical Wools felting on page 114.*

a one-stop reference and resource guide to understanding the materials and terminology of sewing, quilting, and hand embroidery.

Inspiration, anyone?

I've included many colorful samples and art sewing pieces from my personal collection in this book. It might look like quite a hodgepodge of techniques and experiments, but each finished piece represents a stepping-stone in the evolution of my style. I am so energized when I push my art ideas in the direction of using needles, threads, and fabric, and the result still reflects who I am as an artist and carries my unmistakable stamp. You, too, will probably find that in making art with paint, dye, fabric, and thread, the possibilities are endless, and your signature style still shines through! It is truly my hope that this book helps you achieve that result.

Why stitch?

In our highly tech-based society, there is still a need to give attention to the work of the hand, to tactile activity, and to the natural crafting impulses we evolved with as humans.

In my international teaching experience, I have found that people today are drawn to art and stitching as a way to "be in the moment." Our culture is craving human touch and activity that is not dependent on a keyboard, Wi-Fi signal, or cell tower. Will we leave just databases and text messages to future generations? Hopefully not. A legacy of handmade heirlooms would seem more significant in reflecting the human spirit and a full, rich life.

Art to sewing, or sewing to art?

Dip your toes in the stitching or fabric-painting waters to move your creative thoughts and skills deeper. Wherever you are on your creative path, I invite you to step into my art space as I show you a variety of textile ideas and projects that explore handstitching, machine sewing, quilting, embroidery, painting, dyeing, drawing, and lettering. Use this book as an introduction to any or all of these topics. Try a little bit of everything and see where your epiphanies lead you, then dive deeper into the subject matter as your art evolves.

joannesharpe

« *This is an example of my "stitch meditations" (see page 36) I use to start each day.*

MIXED-MEDIA STITCHING BASICS

Before we try out specific mixed-media sewing techniques and jump into making projects, we'll cover some of the background information that will make your journey a successful one, including all of the supplies and tools I use in my stitch art. Chances are you've already dabbled in art or sewing, so some of this information will be a handy review for you. Otherwise, I hope it will be an inspiring and informative springboard for your own art!

THE ART OF THE STITCH

Get ready to explore the abundance of options in mixed-media art stitching. You will draw and paint and stitch, but this need not be a huge leap—think about how you can do this most easily. If you're an artist, you might turn sketches from your journals into patterns and design elements for sewing projects. If you're a quilter or sewing enthusiast, you could strategize how to add fabric paints to your style of stitching. There are so many directions to take this craft, from making painted and hand-dyed fabrics and quilting them on a sewing machine to using a journal sketch as inspiration for simple handstitching with piles of bright, colorful threads.

My approach to whimsical art sewing is by no means meant to be a guide to making someone a master quilter or painter, but is instead meant to inspire a curious creative blending of art and skill. You need have no concern that I will suggest sewing perfect half-square triangles or ¼-inch seams. While I am in complete and total awe of my friends and others who are so disciplined in these skills, that's not me. Taking a curious approach to making any art allows me to try everything in hopes that I will be inspired by one little task, idea, or technique.

Right now you might be saying, "I don't need to take on another craft," and I understand that perfectly well. But if you don't expand your creative horizons, you might just miss that one route you were unaware of that will lead you right where you were meant to

» **Play.** 17½" × 13" (44.5 × 33 cm); dye color, acrylic paint, art pigments; free-motion stitching.

How It Began

I have been sewing since I was a young girl, mesmerized at the side of my grandmother and great-aunt, who could both do anything on a sewing machine. When we got married thirty years ago, my husband and I each took $200 from our wedding money to buy an item for our home that would benefit our future family. I bought a Kenmore sewing machine, and he bought an Atari video game system! I still have that old sewing machine tucked away in a closet as a testament to my roots. As a mom to three boys and one girl, I don't even know how many video game systems we've run through in this house, but there's always been a working sewing machine that has made Halloween costumes, home décor, gifts, and even handmade flags.

For many years, I was a gypsy artist with a very successful business traveling to art shows selling handpainted flags. When I look back, I realize that this was my first venture into mixed-media art sewing. Each 24" × 30" (61 × 76 cm) and 12" × 18" (30.5 × 45.5 cm) piece of special fabric was handpainted with acrylics, making it the perfect waterproof art accessory for a garden. I sold hundreds. My tagline for this product was "Unlike Picasso's, my work hangs on the outside of your house."

» A few of my early explorations in whimiscal stitching.

» **It's Never Too Late.** 12" × 15" (30.5 × 38 cm); hand embroidery. See page 128 for a template you can trace to create this piece.

It's never too late to be what you might have been

GEORGE ELIOT

» **Winged Heart.** 10¾" × 11¾" (27.5 × 30 cm); assorted fabric paints; free-motion machine stitching.

be! Sewing and handstitching are mood-altering, therapeutic, relaxing, stimulating, and tactile. They require a kind of constant, thoughtful motion that is calming. We seem to be hungry for this kind of diversion from our plugged-in lifestyles, and, for some of us, creating with our hands becomes an everyday human need.

Embrace the "art of the stitch," infusing your art with color and texture and combining fabric, threads, and your stash of art supplies. Find yourself in the art zone and abandon the need for perfection. Play, experiment, practice. Get in the rhythm, the repetitive motion of a needle piercing fabric.

Making art with a needle, threads, fabrics, fibers, crayons, pencils, inks, dyes, and paints brings your creative ideas into a completely different dimension. It's exhilarating. For me, whimsical "artful stitching" is a process of exploring the combination of many materials as I continue to grow as an artist. I welcome the challenge of coming up with purposes for my beautiful fabric

paintings and embellished fiber art. Projects can be fabulously functional, such as pillows, totes, pouches, and journal and sketchbook covers, or they might be destined for pure aesthetic enjoyment, such as wall quilts.

As you go through this book, think of yourself as being in an art class. Imagine your elementary school self, all excited to venture into new art territory. As children, we were always encouraged to create with piles of assorted materials, combining elements to express ourselves and make a masterpiece. Give yourself permission to be that curious, uninhibited, enthusiastic kid, using all of your art stuff, fabric, and threads to create an experience, make a dynamic piece, and perhaps discover a new passion.

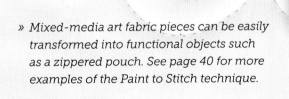

» Mixed-media art fabric pieces can be easily transformed into functional objects such as a zippered pouch. See page 40 for more examples of the Paint to Stitch technique.

THE ART SEWING STUDIO

To make sewing art, you'll need to stock your work area with specific supplies essential for both sewing and art. Before you go out and purchase anything new, review the supply lists that follow, look around your studio, and make an inventory of what you already have. It really isn't necessary to go out and spend tons of money on all new materials, especially if you have some already. In that case, you'll just be learning to use the same supplies in a fresh new way.

On the following pages, you'll see what I have in my art sewing studio and stitching stash. Many of these supplies were already in my art room among my mixed-media materials when I began combining art and sewing, but I did have to learn about and add some of the sewing and quilting items.

To keep order with the different materials in my workspace, I use large decorative trays and little baskets to organize the items according to their purpose, such as tools (scissors, pens, rotary cutter), painting supplies (paints, dyes, brushes), machine-sewing items (thread, needles, bobbins), hand-embroidery supplies (hoops, needles, fibers, threads). A little organization will help keep you from becoming overwhelmed by the different supply categories necessary for mixed-media art sewing.

I'll mention some brand names to guide you in a direction to choosing materials that will give you the best results. All of these items are my personal favorites that I use in my own work. They've been proven to perform, and I recommend them for best results.

BUILD YOUR FABRIC STASH

The first thing you need when creating mixed-media fabric art is fabric! Figuring out what kind of fabric is best for a project can be daunting. You can really get lost in the fabric jungle, with its overwhelming choices and many levels of quality. When purchasing fabric, my experience has always been that you get what you pay for.

Seek out high-quality textiles from brick-and-mortar quilt shops as well as specialty retailers online. When I travel around the country to teach, I always scout out the local quilt and sewing shops.

How much fabric should you buy? That depends on your project, of course, but if you just love a fabric and are shopping to build your stash, always get at least one yard. My quilting friends tell me that "if you really, really love it" and know you can't live without it, you should purchase multiple yards. Fabrics tend to be seasonal, having limited availability because manufacturers constantly add new lines. If you see it and love it, chances are you won't find it readily later in the year—that's been my experience.

Think about the direction in which you'd like take your stitching and textile art. Do you want to create with designer fabrics and cotton quilting collections? Are you drawn to the color palettes and textures of batiks? Are artisan hand-dyed fabrics what you need to capture the look you're after? Here's my shortlist of favorite fabrics for crafting. I always have some on hand, and each has its virtues and strong points. I recommend giving all of them a try to see if they work for your projects.

Muslin

This 100 percent cotton fabric takes paint and inks very well, is inexpensive, and is widely available on the market. It's a workhorse and makes an excellent base for dyeing, painting, quilting, and fusing. I consider muslin the "art paper" in my process of creating textile art. Choose a good-quality muslin because you want it to take dye and paint well. You might start by purchasing small swatches of a few brands to test with your colorants. (Don't forget to label the swatches first!)

» Batiks

» Commercial Quilting Cottons

» Hand-Dyed Textiles

16

PFD Fabric

PFD, or "Prepared for Dyeing," fabric is a cotton made specifically for hand dyeing. I find it a good choice in combination with any inks or paints.

Batiks

Commercial batik fabrics have rich organic patterns, colors, and textures adapted from handprinted art, mainly from Indonesia. I love working with batiks and use them in almost all of my stitching projects, as you'll see throughout this book.

Commercial Quilting Cottons

These collections are created by artists and designers with a heavy trend focus on themes and colorways. They're available in solids, subtle patterns, and bold prints.

Hand-Dyed Textiles

Hand-dyed textiles are the most decadent of all fabrics—sewing with them is like sewing on art. No two pieces are ever the same, and the colors are pure, vibrant, and rich. There are many independent quilt artists who also hand-dye fabric, and Etsy is a good place to find them.

Wool Felt

Real wool felt is far superior to craft felt. Weeks Dye Works makes beautiful hand-dyed wool felt for appliqué and for use as the base for needlefelting projects (see Whimsical Wools, page 114).

» Watch magic appear when you color white tone-on-tone fabric with inks, paints, crayons, and markers. Because it is commercially screened onto the cotton fabric with a waterproof ink, the allover pattern acts as a resist. (See Coloring Blocks, 48, for how to create a similar design to the one shown here.)

A FABRIC COLORING AND PAINTING PALETTE

Different brands and materials of paints, dyes, and markers will give varied results. I am constantly asked what the best products are for art projects. Since there is no one right answer, I always suggest testing, experimenting, and playing with different materials to discover the perfect media for you personally. Keeping in mind your budget, frequency of use, and purpose will be key in deciding what products to add to your art space. I always teach from my personal preferences and direct experience with materials.

Fabric Paints

There are numerous brands of paint that are formulated to work directly on fabric, all with properties and price points that make them unique. In fact, the marketplace can seem overwhelming when you're choosing paint for textiles. Try to find fabric paints that fit your budget and project goals. Before purchasing an entire palette of a particular brand, get one color each of several brands and see which you like best. My personal favorites are SoSoft by DecoArt and Tulip brand, both of which are easy to find in big-box craft stores, and Setacolor by Pebeo

and Lumiere by Jacquard, which are found mostly in fine-art stores.

Acrylic Paints

If you're a mixed-media artist, you almost certainly have collections of assorted acrylic paints in tubes. If acrylics are new to you, though, remember the "try before you buy the whole palette" rule: Purchase one sample each of several brands to see what speaks to you and fits into your personal budget. Since the pigments in acrylic paints are held together with polymers, your fabric will turn stiff when painted unless you add textile medium (see page 20) to soften the finish. Textile medium also makes the paint more permanent.

Fluid Acrylic Paints

Fluid acrylics, which come in bottles, are highly pigmented but thin enough to move around on fabric effortlessly. You'll still have to mix them with textile medium when using them on fabric to reduce stiffness. To me, the way these paints move over fabric so easily makes them feel like a cross between water-color paints and acrylics.

» *Some of my must-have paints and dyes. Most of my fabric art projects begin with these mediums.*

Tips for Coloring Fabric

Wash fabrics before applying paints, dyes, markers, or pencils. Fabrics are manufactured with various amounts of sizing, a starch-like substance added to material to reduce fiber breakage. Sizing can interfere with the total absorption of your paints and mediums and should be washed out first.

When applying color, lay fabric on the shiny side of freezer paper so the paint doesn't stick to other surfaces. Use packing tape to connect sheets of freezer paper for larger pieces of fabric.

Keep an assortment of brushes designated for different techniques for fabric.

Paint several large pieces (18"x 24" [45.5 x 61 cm] and larger) at a time to supply your fabric stash with handmade pieces to use in future projects.

Mediums

A medium is a substance that is added to paint to change the consistency or create other effects. Here are two I keep in my painting kit.

Textile Mediums

There are many brands of textile, or fabric, mediums to choose from, but all achieve the same results: they enhance the workability and movement of paint on fabric, penetrating the fabric fibers to control bleeding and reduce the stiffness of the dried paint for a softer feel. Heat setting is not needed. Choose the product that fits your budget. Test your textile medium and paints on practice fabric before you begin your projects. My brands of choice for textile mediums are Liquitex and Golden.

No Flow Medium

I recently discovered this great product by Jacquard that, when applied to fabric, keeps dye and paint from bleeding extensively. Apply No Flow to muslin or cotton fabrics and let dry overnight. Markers, paints, dye colors, and pigments will remain stable with very minimal or no bleed.

Dye-Na-Flow

This paint by Jacquard is a clean, crisp colorant that acts like dye.

Spray Dyes and Inks

There are many brands of spray dyes and inks on the market, such as SEI Tumble Dye and Tulip Tie-Dye. They all work well, but check labels for settings and permanency.

Inktense Pencils and Blocks

Derwent Inktense Pencils deposit pure, intense color onto paper and fabric. These unique colored pencils are infused with brilliant dye pigments that are water-reactive. The harder you press one of these pencils into fabric fibers, the more intense the color appears in your image.

Watercolor Crayons

Watercolor crayons are pure color pigment in crayon form, combining drawing and painting and easily covering large areas of fabric. Ultrarich, highly concentrated, creamy pigments are drawn and pressed into fabric and then activated with water. I achieve the most success using Caran d'Ache Neocolor II and Daniel Smith Extra Fine Watercolor Sticks.

Art Markers

If you're an art-supply hoarder (I mean, *collector*) like me, you probably have a healthy marker stash. Just remember that all markers are not created equal! Experiment with all your pens and markers to see how they react on fabric. You'll be amazed at the spectrum of results. Become familiar with the specific types of pens you own, as well as the distinctive inks.

Dye-Based Ink Art Markers

Dye-based art markers such as those from Tombow (my preferred brand to use on fabric) react to water and won't bleed through paper. They will, however, bleed through fabric as the ink penetrates the woven fibers that are looser than the pressed fibers of paper. You can get a spectacular watercolor effect on fabric and paper with Tombow Dual Brush Pens, drawing with color, then activating with water. But use them only for decorative art—they're not washable.

Fabric Markers

There are several brands of markers made just for coloring on fabric. They can be heat-set to make them permanent.

Alcohol Markers

This type of marker deposits color combined with alcohol or solvent onto a surface. Caution: it will always bleed through paper and fibers. Prismacolor, Copic, and Sharpie all make alcohol markers.

Pigment Marker Pens

Pigment marker pens, such as the ones from Faber-Castell Pitt, Zig, and Sakura, contain color pigment in concentrated formulas that will penetrate fabric fibers but not bleed or

« *Markers, watercolor crayons, and pens create wonderful designs on fabric. Some are applied dry and activated with water.*

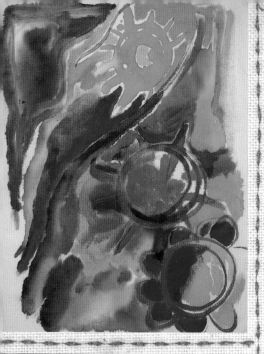

Dyeing Fabrics

While I am very intrigued by the idea of dyeing my own fabric, I don't do it. It's an involved process that requires specific materials, chemical mixing, and a designated workspace. There are many talented artists and quilting friends who sell their handpainted fabrics, and I'm happy to support them and honor their work by purchasing their fabrics. Etsy and other websites are a good resource for finding artists who hand-dye fabric. If this is something you're "dyeing" to pursue, seek out books and specialized workshops to learn more.

Intuitive Fabric Paintings

What could be more authentic than creating your own hand-painted fabric, then using it to make fiber art?

Use plain, natural muslin, PFD (Prepared for Dye) fabric, commercial cottons in solid colors and prints, and vintage textiles as your painting and coloring "canvas." After you have collected fabrics to transform, dig deep into your mixed-media supplies and experiment with simple dyes, paints, inks, markers, pencils, and crayons.

To always be ready when the stitching urge strikes, keep stacks of foundation fabrics ready to build on and make artwork on fabric for your whimsical stitching.

« *Freeform fabric paintings make wonderful bases for mixed-media art sewing projects.*

spread. Pigment pens are the perfect choice for drawing your own designs on fabric for needlework and embroidery.

Color Pigments

One of my favorite art products is pure color pigment—powdered color infused with mica pigments that you combine with textile medium and apply to fabric. They'll give your textile art a little extra "bling."

THREAD-CETERA

Whether you're sewing on a machine, stitching by hand, or embroidering embellishments, good-quality thread can make or break your project—literally!

Machine-Sewing Thread

I always work with 40-weight and 50-weight threads. A good-quality thread will give you the best results. My machine threads of choice are Aurifil, Floriani, Isacord, and Superior.

Embroidery Threads

As you venture deeper into the art of embroidery and handstitching, you will find that there are many excit-

ing (or possibly overwhelming) choices for threads and fibers. When starting out, put together a small collection of basic threads and floss in your favorite colors, stored in a way that's easy to access.

Embroidery Floss

Six-stranded cotton embroidery floss is easily separated into different strands for various thicknesses and line weight of stitching. My favorite brands include Aurifil, Weeks Dye Works, and DMC.

» **Happy.** 7½" (19 cm). Paint a simple sketch with watercolor on white muslin fabric and secure in a wooden embroidery hoop. Use hand embroidery and colorful threads to outline and give dimension to the painting.

On Display

At a workshop at Judith Baker Montano's art studio I learned the most ingenious way to store embroidery threads. She unwinds the skeins and loops them around assorted-size embroidery hoops. This system keeps the threads easily accessible and free from tangling, and hanging the hoops in your art space creates quite a display of eye candy.

You can arrange the threads in color families or like a color wheel to conveniently choose materials for specific projects.

Pearl Cotton

Pearl (sometimes called perle) cotton is a silkier single-strand, twisted thread that comes in a shank or ball in a variety of colors and thicknesses, from #3, the thickest, to #12, the thinnest. I mostly use Valdani #8 and DMC #3, #5, and #8. I prefer pearl cotton over embroidery floss because I like the thickness and presence it has in a project.

Silk

Although a little costly, these beautiful hand-dyed, extra-fine threads have a soft hand and the slight shimmer of silk.

Metallic

You can buy embroidery threads and fine yarns with metallic fibers woven through the strands. These threads are lovely for adding sparkle and bling to a project.

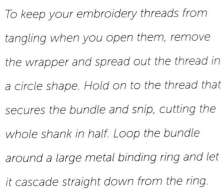

{TIP}

To keep your embroidery threads from tangling when you open them, remove the wrapper and spread out the thread in a circle shape. Hold on to the thread that secures the bundle and snip, cutting the whole shank in half. Loop the bundle around a large metal binding ring and let it cascade straight down from the ring.

Threads and floss for sewing, quilting, and handstitching come in myriad colors, including variegated shades.

Basic Embroidery Stitches

When you revisit or start your embroidery journey, you'll learn that there are hundreds of combinations of stitches to use in needlework. Since my process is to illustrate my own art and doodles on fabric, I choose very basic handstitches for my pieces. Stitching requires knowledge of pattern and form, repetition, and a personal rhythm that comes with practice. To master various stitches, make a stitch-sampler practice book for your personal reference. Try inventing your own handstitching patterns by combining several basic stitches in an interesting collage in thread.

The basic embroidery stitches can be broken down into groups:

Outline Stitches

- Straight/running stitch, backstitch, stem stitch, chain stitch

Decorative Stitches

- Seed stitch, lazy daisy stitch, feather stitch, fly stitch, chevron stitch, French knots

Filler Stitch

- Satin stitch

Texture Stitch

- Couching stitch

(See page 138 for how-tos of the embroidery stitches used throughout this book.)

ARTFUL SUPPLIES AND TOOLS

When I was in school, I loved shopping for new school supplies. Stocking up on pencils, brushes, and other basic art supplies gives me the same feeling of a fresh start.

Composition Book

Buy an inexpensive student-grade composition book for quick sketches and for brainstorming stitching ideas.

Sketchbook or Art Journal

I use a journal with better-quality paper to flesh out my ideas before starting a project.

Colored Pencils

I use Prismacolor brand colored pencils to color my sketches of stitching designs.

Sharpie Black Pen

A standard fine-point Sharpie is a necessity for sketching.

Pencil and Eraser

Always have these on hand for capturing inspiration.

Waterproof Pigment Ink Pens

Fine-tip black or sepia pens by Faber-Castell Pitt or Sakura Pigma Micron are my go-to tools for sketching and drawing directly on fabric.

Lightbox

This is a great tool that replaces the awkward process of tracing on a lighted window. I

» *Stock up on some basic art supplies for sketching and planning projects, as well as for creative textile techniques.*

have an Artograph, and it's perfect for transferring designs onto fabric and paper.

Brushes

Understanding the features of specific brush types will alleviate stress and frustration as you work. With the hundreds of specialty brushes available, selecting the right ones can seem next to impossible, but art-store staff can assist you in choosing brushes most appropriate for textiles. Use soft-bristle watercolor brushes for your flowing dye paints and inks. A stiffer brush is necessary for working with heavier acrylic paints and mediums. Specialty fabric-painting brushes or acrylic paintbrushes are best for this.

Water Brush

The Yasutomo Niji Waterbrush and Pentel Arts Aquash Brush hold water in their barrels that you squeeze to dispense as you paint. They are great for on-the-go painting, as you don't have to carry a water container.

Watercolor Paintbrushes

In my studio, I use round #4, #8, #10, #12, and ¾" (2 cm) flat brushes.

Fabric Paintbrushes

Find brushes with stiffer bristles for working with heavier mediums—acrylic paintbrushes or specific fabric-painting brushes work well. Tulip-brand brushes are easy to find in stores, inexpensive, and excellent for fabric painting.

Cosmetic Wedges

Use these for applying acrylic paints or dyes to paper or fabric, as well as for stenciling.

Art Stencils

There are several companies that market stencils with hundreds of patterns and designs. StencilGirl, The Crafter's Workshop, and Artistcellar are a few that feature contemporary, on-trend, and highly artistic designs.

» **Stenciled Pouch.** *10½" × 7" (26.5 × 18 cm) (closed); dye colors; stenciling, free-motion stitching. See Stencil and Sew (page 68) for more ideas on incorporating stenciling into your pieces.*

The Make & Play Art Sampler

Applying paints, dyes, and other mediums to fabric can be tricky, so it's helpful to know what materials you have and what they can do.

Make a cloth sampler book using a variety of supplies on 6" × 6" (15 × 15 cm) sheets of plain muslin, PFD fabric, and prints. Sew cloth pages together with batting in the middle to try out all your supplies on the fabrics. Think of this sampler as an art journal for textile art. Most of these materials will be used for decorative art only and would most likely wash out of fabric.

Break out your whole mixed-media supply stash. Try out your basic acrylic and fluid acrylic paints with textile medium. Color a simple image with Inktense pencils, watercolor paints, watercolor crayons and pencils, or Tombow markers and activate with water. Test fabric markers, liquid dyes, mica paints, pigment powders, and watercolor stamping inks on fabric.

Apply each product onto the fabric pages in an organized fashion. Label the brand and specific product with a fine-tip permanent pen, under the colored swatch.

Note the unique characteristics of each product and how you might find use for the various effects in textile artwork.

"Primary Elements"
ARTIST
PIGMENTS*

SKY BLUE

SPICED PUMPKIN

So many paints...
So many inks...
So many pens....
So little time!

KEY LIME

*TRY EVERYTHING!

MON OP

TEAL ZIRCON

GINGER FLOWER

mixed with textile medium

Golden Fluid Acrylic

Golden Fluid Acrylic with Fabric medium

straight paint on fabric

Tulip brand fabric paint

k-sharpie pen

CraftFlow acrylic

Jacquard Textile Color

Setacolor Fabric Paints (OPAQUE)

Ranger Distress Paints

Golden over Ranger acrylic

Sharpie Pen ULTRA FINE POINT

SHARPIE PEN

an d'ache   NEOCOLOR II
WATERCOLOR CRAYONS

Rac-Lok muslin

* color dry, add water

...fabric medium treated...
MEDIUM PAINTED ON FABRIC

ink acrylic black

(writing over Golden Fluid Paint with sharpie marker)

Dye-Na-Flow
...color intensity is diluted, not as vibrant as it is on raw fabric

SHARPIE PEN

MARKER TEST: (fabric med

TOMBOW

...beautiful wash created on fabric medium treated fabric. Color with marker then add water

Copic MARKER

KOI COLOR BRUSH

...soft diluted color, nice watercolor effect.

sharpie pen over Koi

ICY
YE
NS

FABRIC marker by Fabrico

*TRY DIFFERENT GRADES OF MUSLIN and COTTON FABRICS

love this fine tip for writing

o brand

SHARPIE PEN

Watercolor Paints - RAW FABRIC

(color very muted)

SHARPIE PEN
ULTRA FINE POINT

Watercolor Paints - "NO FLOW" TREATED FABRIC

Art makes your soul VISIBLE

(more intense color)   (SHARPIE PEN)

STITCHING MUST-HAVES

These are the tools and supplies I consider necessary for a well-stocked sewing room.

Sewing Machine

You're only going to want to sew if you have a reliable machine in good working order. I find that one of the biggest frustrations with some machines is the inability to lower the feed dogs—a must for free-motion sewing (see page 42). I'm a BERNINA girl all the way. I currently have a 790 model.

Straight-Stitch Sewing Foot

The basic foot that usually comes on a sewing machine, it's used for sewing straight lines, seams, bindings, and borders.

Darning Foot

The most important tool for free-motion sewing, the darning foot allows you to move your fabric under the needle effortlessly without engaging the feed dogs. Make sure you have the correct foot specifically designed for your brand of sewing machine.

Sewing Machine Needles

Use a universal 80/12 needle, which has a slight ball point for basic sewing and piecing. A 90/14 quilting needle has a sharp point to prevent damage to fabric sewn in layers and is best for topstitching designs and quilting motifs.

Chenille Handsewing Needles

The proper needles are crucial to art stitching. A chenille needle has a large eye for thicker threads and a sharper point to penetrate painted fabrics.

Rotary Cutter

This is a must-have tool for cutting straight lines in fabric.

Cutting Mat

A mat has a numbered grid for measuring and is used with a rotary cutter.

Clear Quilting Ruler

Use with a rotary cutter on a cutting mat for making straight lines and pieces.

Batting

Standard 80/20 or 100 percent cotton quilt battings are sandwiched between layers of fabric to give shape to art pieces.

Fusible Interfacing

Featherweight and lightweight interfacing are usually used for garment construction. I find they are perfect for stabilizing fabric for my stitching projects.

Polyester Fiberfill

You can find this loose stuffing for dimensional fabric projects in fabric and craft stores.

» *Essential tools you'll need for machine and handsewing.*

All About Quilt Batting

Batting is used to give a piece more body, shape, texture, and dimension. The techniques and projects in this book often start with a "quilt sandwich," made by placing batting between two pieces of fabric. Different types of batting will provide different results in your projects.

Cotton batting—my favorite for most quilts and other stitched projects as it drapes beautifully and is soft and warm.

Cotton/polyester-blend batting—similar to cotton batting but lighter (good for large quilts); choose one with a higher proportion of cotton so it doesn't break down easily.

100 percent wool—provides a puffy, raised trapunto (stuffed) effect.

Wool felt—a nice alternative to traditional batting as a base for quilting.

Soft and Stable—a brand of batting from ByAnnie's that is almost foamlike and is used to give structure to bags; its high loft makes it a great base for art quilts and other pieces that require sewing around shapes.

Embroidery Hoops

These come in many sizes. I usually stitch in a 5" (12.5 cm) or 7" (18 cm) hoop for ease of movement.

Fabric Scissors

Designate specific scissors for your fabric and stitching projects. In my studio and workshops, you'll always find scissors by my favorite makers, Havel's and Karen Kay Buckley. Never cut anything besides fabric with your fabric scissors to keep them sharp.

Embroidery Scissors

Invest in a little pair of embroidery scissors for snipping threads.

Paper Scissors

Keep a separate pair of scissors for paper cutting, as paper will quickly dull fabric scissors.

Freezer Paper

Found in grocery stores, basic Reynolds Freezer Paper is used for making paper templates.

» *Three Flowers.* 12" × 13" (30.5 × 33 cm); dye color; free-motion quilting. This is an example of the Paint to Stitch technique (see page 40).

» *Heart Journal.* 6" × 8" (15 × 20.5 cm) (closed); dyed color, free-motion stitching, hand embroidery. See page 64 for instructions on a making a similar handsewn journal or sketchbook.

Fusible Web Interfacing

Fusible web is an essential art-sewing studio staple used for "gluing" fabric components together for appliqué or collage. I use Misty-fuse and Lite Steam-A-Seam 2. (See page 76 for more on using fusible web.)

Transdoodle

Made by Mistyfuse, this is an excellent re-usable coated paper for transferring designs and lettering onto fabric.

Disappearing Ink Fabric Pen

Various manufacturers such as Dritz and Singer produce pens for marking, lettering, and drawing on fabric without leaving traces afterward. Depending on the product, lines and marks usually wipe away with water or friction.

Pins

Keep straight sewing pins and small safety pins handy to arrange project components and patterns.

Iron

Any domestic steam iron will work fine for your pressing needs.

{TIP}

Embroidery can be a great travel project. I use a zippered pouch to store my handstitching supplies so everything is extremely portable.

Don't Fear the Sewing Machine!

All too often I hear from my mixed-media art students that "I can't even thread a machine!" If that's your story, it's an easy fix. Just learn the basic mechanics of your personal machine. This is the one tool that can change your creative life, as it did mine. And make sure you have a decent sewing maching that will perform for you, not make you tear your hair out. After years of cursing the several inexpensive machines I purchased for my art, I finally invested in a high-quality BERNINA sewing machine. I heard angels sing as I watched every perfect stitch spill out. I sew every single day, so a good machine was a great investment for me. There are so many options for machines on the market today, and it can be daunting trying to figure out what you'll need. Go to your local sewing machine shops and ask your friends for their opinions on the brands they own. For me, a sewing machine that I can count on is one of the most important tools for mixed-media art sewing.

CHOOSING COLOR STORIES

Students constantly ask me, "What colors should I use?" I usually suggest buying the colors of fabric, fibers, and paints that speak to them personally. I am obviously a bright-colors kind of girl, and I love color in my art and in every aspect of my life. I will always choose turquoise, lime green, orange, hot pink, and violet, as well as black and white. If you like prefer a more neutral palette, choose those colors. You need to be passionately in love with your color choices because that energy and intention will be evident and come out in your work.

Even though I personally take the "just go with it" approach, using colors that speak to me at a particular moment in time in making art, as a teacher I empower students with the skills to make choices that will result in successful and pleasing artwork.

When planning your stitching projects, use the color wheel to choose "color stories" that will inspire color harmony in your artwork. It's helpful to review and to be confident with the principles of the color wheel and understand how to arrange color in an aesthetically pleasing way.

Color Theory 101

The three colors that combine to form all other colors are yellow, red, and blue. They're called the *primary colors*. If you mix paints, inks, or dyes in all three of these colors you will get a brown color.

Mixing two primaries creates a *secondary color*. Red plus yellow makes orange; red and blue form violet; and blue and yellow make green.

Combining the secondary colors produces *tertiary colors* (red-orange, blue-green, etc.).

Tints are colors with white added to the base (e.g., red + white = pink), and *shades* have black added (e.g., red + black = burgundy).

When buying paint, dyes, fabric, and threads, start with the three primary colors (yellow, red, blue) and the three secondary colors (orange, violet, green). (You can make your own secondary colors, but it's easier to buy them.) Add to the basic palette whatever tints (white added to any of the colors that make pastel colors) and shades (black added to any of the colors that make darker tones) you love.

Colorful Combinations

Here are some tried-and-true color combos you might want to use in your artwork.

To create harmony, try colors that are all tints or all shades in a piece.

Use three colors that appear in a sequence on the color wheel (called *analogous* colors) for another harmonious option.

Colors that are across from each (think red and green) are *complementary* colors. Using them together creates contrast. Try adding just a touch of a complementary color to add pop.

Use warm- (yellows, reds, oranges) or cool- (blue, violet, greens) themed color palettes in your stitch projects for dramatic visuals.

Stitch a Color Wheel

On plain white muslin fabric, make a reference color wheel using fabric scraps, embroidery threads, paints, and dyes. As you arrange and stitch the color order, you will get a clear understanding of how color can be chosen for visual appeal. Cut up a color wheel and rearrange the pieces into endless color story combinations. Just play with color and enjoy the process.

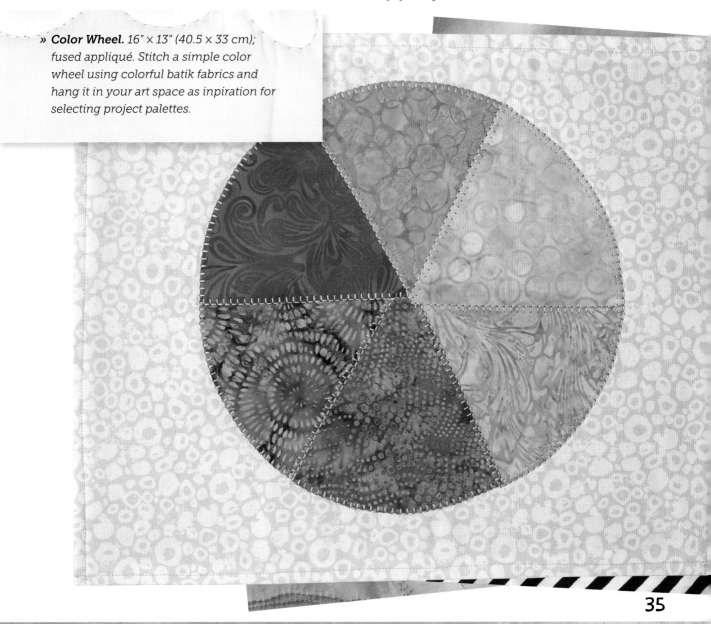

» **Color Wheel.** *16" × 13" (40.5 × 33 cm); fused appliqué. Stitch a simple color wheel using colorful batik fabrics and hang it in your art space as inpiration for selecting project palettes.*

Daily Stitch Meditations

Handstitching is a soothing, meditative activity that provides a physical state of peacefulness and calm. The daily practice of stitching can provide uninterrupted moments of thought, meditation, perhaps even prayer. My daily art activities often involve a simple stitching project with no particular end result in mind. Each day, I take 15 to 45 minutes to just "stitch to stitch" to center myself with fabric and threads. My mini stitchings are examples of freeform abstract art. This is also the perfect portable activity for travel, vacations, waiting at appointments, or other idle time. A tactile activity is a wonderful alternative to being attached to an electronic device.

With no project demands or expectations, create small scrap-fabric samplers embellished with an assortment of simple handstitches. Cut colorful scrap fabric into organic or geometric shapes and, with a glue stick, layer them onto a small fabric background, no larger than 8" x 10" (20.5 x 25.5 cm).

Outline and embellish each shape with simple embroidery stitches and matching or contrasting colored embroidery floss or pearl cotton. Basic stitches such as straight stitch, blanket stitch, seed stitch, and French knots are enough to energize a playful composition.

At the start, these little fabric collages should have no intended purpose other than to provide an opportunity to make a textile art experience. These little masterpieces can be sewn into a fabric book or textile journal as examples of various stitching and fabric color combinations.

I'm fascinated with the newly established "Slow Stitching Movement" started by Mark Lipinski. With Mark's permission, from the website slowstitching.com, the concept is described as: "Quick, fast, easy. In our busy, multitasking world, those buzzwords capture our attention. But speed can kill creativity and the enjoyment of our creative pursuits. Maybe what we really need to do is slow down, enjoy the process, and create fiber art that we're really proud of."

» *Three of my meditative mini-stitch masterpieces.*

Part 2

WHIMSICAL TECHNIQUES & FUNK-TIONAL PROJECTS

Now that you have all of your supplies and tools assembled and have spent some time playing with them, you're ready to learn some specific techniques for creating fabric art. Here, I share twelve of my favorites, each with a project for a fun and funky functional item you can make. There are so many possibilities for mixed-media sewing art. As far as I'm concerned, there aren't enough hours in a day to make everything I can dream up.

PAINT TO STITCH

If you've painted on paper or canvas (or even if you haven't), you can paint on fabric! Taking a paintbrush loaded with paint to plain fabric like it's a blank canvas is artistically liberating. When making textile art, I use watercolor paintbrushes and start drawing directly on the fabric with vivid fabric paints, dyes, inks, and even thinned-down acrylic paint. Watching color saturate the fabric fibers is magical to me, as the loose, freehand brushwork makes colorful, wispy watercolor effects. For this technique, I use my sewing machine to trace and accentuate the organic lines, shapes, and images I've painted. The images come to life as the threads create movement and motion. You can start with abstract images or recognizable shapes and motifs, such as flowers.

{TIP}

If you're nervous about painting directly on your fabric, sketch your basic images first with chalk or a water-soluble fabric pen, which will dissolve when you add your water-based paints or dyes.

» **Hearts and Flowers.**
*12" × 8" (30.5 × 20.5 cm);
dye color; free-motion stitching.*

You Will Need

- Plain white or natural-colored muslin
- Cotton batting
- Fabric paint, acrylic paint, or Dye-Na-Flow dyes
- Watercolor paintbrush
- Sewing machine with darning foot
- Machine-sewing thread

The Process

1 Cut a piece of plain white or natural-colored muslin of any size to serve as your canvas. Lay the fabric on top of cotton batting.

2 Using fabric paint, thinned acrylics, or Dye-Na-Flow dyes and a watercolor paintbrush, paint your basic shapes or design on your fabric *(Figure 1)*.

3 Continue filling in your design until you're satisfied *(Figure 2)*.

4 Use free-motion stitching (see page 42) to showcase the lines and characteristics of the painted piece *(Figure 3)*.

FIGURE 1

FIGURE 2

FIGURE 3

Art in Free Motion

Free-motion sewing, in which you "draw" with a sewing machine, is the most thrilling style of art stitching for me. If you can doodle and draw with a pen or pencil, you can conquer free-motion stitching. Instead of a writing instrument, the sewing machine needle becomes a drawing tool.

The needle and thread are my pens and pencils as I move the fabric in any direction, creating organic lines and shapes. I get absorbed in creative bliss.

What You'll Need

Get organized with the right supplies before you start so you can lose yourself in stitching.

Fabric

Start with a "quilt sandwich": two pieces of fabric with batting in between. This is your basic staple canvas for many of the techniques and projects in this book.

Threads

As you're learning to master free-motion sewing, try a variety of threads in your machine, such as 40 weight (abbreviated "wt") and 50 weight. Cotton or cotton-polyester blends are the best choices. I use Aurifil 50 weight (it comes on an orange spool) and Isacord 50 weight (which comes on a green spool). Use the same thread in your bobbin.

Presser Foot

You'll need a darning foot for your machine.

Feed Dogs

Make sure you lower the feed dogs on your machine so that the fabric and needle can move freely as you stitch.

Needles

A Microtex 80/12 universal needle or 90/14 topstitch quilting needle are the best choices for this sewing method. For best results, change your sewing machine needles after every 4 to 6 hours of sewing. A fresh needle is imperative for good stitch quality and to keep your machine running smoothly.

Practice Movement

Start by getting comfortable with the movements of this stitching process by practicing with a pen on paper. Use an inexpensive composition book to draw pages and pages of practice designs that you can translate into stitches on an art quilt. Without lifting your pen off the paper, draw repeating lines that echo each other or that surround a motif. Your muscle memory from writing on the paper will kick in when you're on the sewing machine, and the movements will flow more smoothly over the fabric.

Relax

The key to getting comfortable with free-motion stitching is to relax, breathe, and gently go with the flow of how your fabric and hands are moving in tandem to create a seamless design. You'll find your own personal rhythm with practice, practice, practice!

Keep Stitching

✳ Instead of starting with plain fabric, try this technique on lightly patterned fabrics to add more depth and detail to your artwork.

✳ Embellish the image with decorative hand or machine stitches using colorful threads, embroidery floss, or yarns.

✳ Instead of using your machine to quilt around the images, you can handstitch with straight stitches for a more rustic or organic look.

✳ Create a unique piece of whimsical wall art by framing your stitched piece or adding a fabric border (page 132) and a quilt sleeve (page 135) and hanging it.

» **Not a Placemat.** *19" × 14" (48.5 × 35.5 cm); dye color; free-motion stitching, hand embroidery, decorative machine stitching.*

You Will Need

- Plain white or natural-colored muslin or PFD fabric
- Cotton batting
- Sewing machine with darning foot
- Machine-sewing thread
- Markers, water-soluble crayons, water-soluble pencils, fabric paint, dyes, or fluid acrylic paints

The Process

1   Take two equal-size pieces of plain muslin or PFD fabric and layer with a piece of same-size cotton batting in between to make a "quilt sandwich."

2   Sew to color! Practice the art of free-motion stitching directly on fabric (see page 42), quilting decorative shapes and designs *(Figure 1)*.

3   Color the sewn images with markers (Tombow Dual Brush or fabric markers), water-soluble crayons (Caran d'Ache), and water-soluble pencils (Inktense), fabric paints (SoSoft), dye color (Dye-Na-Flow), or fluid acrylic paints (any brand) *(Figure 2)*.

{TIP}

Make a stockpile of quilt sandwiches for stitching practice.

FIGURE 1

FIGURE 2

» **Shine.** 16½" × 17½" (42 × 44.5 cm); fabric paint, pigment powders, dye color; free-motion stitching.

» **Create.** 7½" × 12" (19 × 30.5 cm); Tombow Dual Brush markers; free-motion stitching, edges finished with hand-stitched blanket stitch.

Keep Stitching

※ Use a variety of different-colored threads for some subtle color play.

※ Try stitching geometric shapes, such as squares and triangles, to create your own piece of modern art!

※ After painting your fabric, accentuate the stitching or add texture with hand embroidery.

» *Ferns and Flowers.* 6¼" × 9" (16 × 23 cm); water-activated Intense pencils; free-motion stitching.

FLOWER POP
Sculpted Pillow

Materials
- 20" × 20" (51 × 51 cm) piece of muslin for top of pillow
- Cotton batting or ByAnnie's Soft and Stable
- 50-weight cotton or polyester thread
- Watercolor crayons
- Caran d'Ache crayons, Inktense pencils, or Tombow markers
- 20" × 20" (51 × 51 cm) piece of batik fabric for back of pillow
- Polyester fiberfill

Tools
- Water-soluble quilting pen
- Sewing machine with darning foot
- Paintbrush or water brush
- Handsewing needle

Finished Size
- About 14" × 14" (35.5 × 35.5 cm)

Bring the outdoors inside with this colorful piece of soft sculpture "couch art." A larger-than-life flower is an easy shape on which to practice freeform stitching. Just think how fun three or four of these pillows would look playfully mimicking a garden on your sofa.

PAINT THE PILLOW FRONT

1 Lay the 20" × 20" (51 × 51 cm) piece of muslin on top of the quilt batting or Soft and Stable (Soft and Stable will create a more raised texture).

2 With a water-soluble quilting pen, draw a simple outline of a daisy shape almost as large as the muslin, stopping about 3" (7.5 cm) from the edge (Figure 1).

3 Start in the middle of your surface and start "drawing" the flower center in a circular motion using free-motion sewing (see page 42). Think of the needle as a pen and get into a rhythm that moves the needle and fabric at a smooth pace. Draw the petals, using soft curves so that the design will turn inside out smoothly when you're ready to make the dimensional shape. You don't want the space in between the petals to be too bulky and pull the fabric.

4 When you're satisfied with your design and image, start coloring with watercolor crayons. Press the pigment from the crayon into the fibers as you color and, with a wet paintbrush or water brush, wet the color and move it around like it's paint. Color the shapes and patterns with Tombow markers or water-reactive pencils and crayons such as Inktense and Caran d'Ache.

SEW THE PILLOW

5 After your image is colored, sew the painted piece and the 20" × 20" (51 × 51 cm) piece of batik fabric with right sides together, stitching ½" (1.3 cm) around the flower shape (what I call "shadow stitching") and leaving a 3" (7.5 cm) opening for adding the stuffing (Figure 2).

6 Trim the piece into the flower shape with soft curves (Figure 3), leaving about ¼" (6 mm) outside the stitching line.

7 Carefully clip across any points and along curves just to, but not through, the stitching line (Figure 4).

8 Turn the piece inside out, push out the petal shapes, and stuff the entire shape with polyester fiberfill.

9 Handstitch the opening closed and watch your garden grow!

FIGURE 1

3" (7.5 cm) opening

FIGURE 2

FIGURE 3

FIGURE 4

DECORATIVE MACHINE DOODLES

Many sewing machines come with banks of decorative stitches, but most sewists never use them. This is your chance to actually use all of those fabulous and sometimes mysterious stitches.

The decorative-art possibilities for these stitches are endless. Think of your stitches as "drawing lines," making intricately patterned doodles on plain fabric to create an elaborate textured surface loaded with detail and interest. Use the machine to draw and embroider artwork or patterns with colorful threads and fabric.

{TIP}

Make sure you have the proper foot on your machine for decorative stitching, My BERNINA machine uses an open-toe embroidery foot to allow for the movements the needle makes when it creates the details of a specific stitch.

« **Swirls and Stitches.** *9½" × 15" (24 × 38 cm). For this art-quilt wall hanging, I used one color of metallic thread to showcase the assorted stitches and add a little bling.*

You Will Need

- Fabric
- Interfacing or stabilizer
- Sewing machine with embroidery foot
- Machine-sewing thread

The Process

1   Stabilize the back of your fabric with interfacing or commercial stabilizer to keep the machine-stitch sequences flat and even. If your fabric is too light or flimsy, the stitches will pull and form irregular patterns, break threads, and make a frustrating mess!

2   Play and practice with the decorative stitches, moving the patterns in curved lines or simple shapes (Figures 1–3).

Keep Stitching

✳ Stitch line patterns on handpainted fabric, then wrap and staple around a small canvas to make textile wall art.

✳ Paint small pieces of muslin quilt sandwiches to make ornaments or gift tags. Use machine stitches to decorate and embellish.

✳ Add paint, pigments, and markers to color in the shapes created with the decorative stitching.

✳ Paint, color, or dye your imagery first, then embellish the artwork with decorative stitches. Sew up a sampler piece showcasing all the decorative stitches on your personal machine.

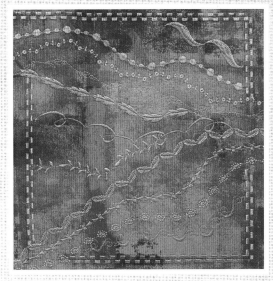

FIGURE 1

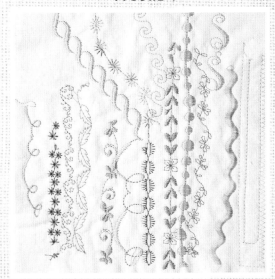

FIGURE 2

FIGURE 3

FANCY QUILTED
pouch

Materials

- 10" × 14" (25.5 × 35.5 cm) piece of fabric for outside of pouch
- 10" × 14" (25.5 × 35.5 cm) piece of fusible featherweight interfacing
- Assorted machine threads
- Cotton batting
- 10" × 14" (25.5 × 35.5 cm) piece of fabric for lining
- 22" × 2" (56 × 5 cm) piece of cotton fabric for binding
- Decorative button

Tools

- Iron
- Sewing machine that can sew decorative stitches
- Embroidery foot

Finished Size

- 9½" × 6" (24 × 15 cm)

You can never have too many places to stash your art supplies, stitching projects, cosmetics, or high-tech gadgets. Creating the elaborately textured fabric of this pouch is so much fun and the construction is so simple, you'll find yourself making bunches of them in no time. Just fold over the top for easy access to the contents. Fancy that!

Make the Quilted Fabric

1. Iron fusible featherweight interfacing to the wrong side of the outside fabric.

2. Sew decorative stitches from the top to the bottom of your outer fabric. You could sew in a straight line or move your fabric gently to form undulating lines and movement *(Figure 1)*. Use a variety of stitches and thread colors.

3. Make a quilt sandwich with the stitched piece, batting, and lining fabric. With a plain straight stitch, stitch in between the decorative lines with contrasting thread to quilt the pouch fabric *(Figure 2)*.

Assemble the Pouch

4. Sew binding to the two short edges of the quilted fabric (see page 132). Do some decorative machine stitching on top of attached binding (I chose a different design for each binding).

5. Fold top of bound piece down 2" (5 cm) right side to right side *(Figure 3)*.

6. Fold up bottom about 6" (15 cm) so bottom binding is flush with top fold *(Figure 4)*.

7. Sew each side with a ¼" (6 mm) seam from top to bottom *(Figure 5)*.

8. Gently turn the pouch inside out and push out the corner points. The seaming

» *Use a contrasting fabric for the inside of the pouch for a pop of fun color.*

creates a self-closing fold over the top flap.

9 Steam-press the entire piece so the pouch lies flat and smooth. Add a decorative button to the front flap.

{TIP}

Have a practice piece of stabilized fabric to test your stitches on. This will allow you to make decisions before you move on to your "good fabric." Try the stitches and create a scrap sampler so you're familiar with how each stitch looks and how long it takes to complete.

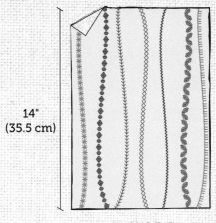

14"
(35.5 cm)

FIGURE 1

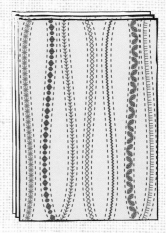

FIGURE 2

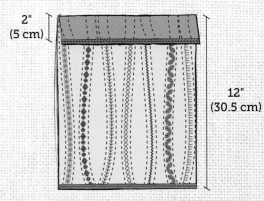

2"
(5 cm)

12"
(30.5 cm)

FIGURE 3

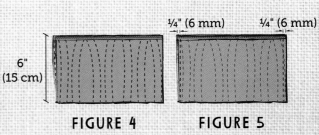

¼" (6 mm)   ¼" (6 mm)

6"
(15 cm)

FIGURE 4   **FIGURE 5**

DOODLE HANDSTITCHING

I actually get excited little butterflies in my stomach anticipating a handstitching and embroidery project. There is something about this craft that is so tranquil and essential to my creative bliss. It brings my blood pressure way down. I find that in the midst of business- and technology-driven everyday chaos, I long for a quiet way of life that is simple and soulful. In the right setting, stitching can be a form of reflection, meditation, and prayer.

Doodle stitching is just using threads and embroidery floss to create random, free-flowing lines and patterns to embellish textile art—a perfectly meditative practice.

Relax and try to settle into a stream of consciousness mode when stitching. Let the stitches lead you.

A playful way to practice and master multiple hand-embroidery stitches is to make a stitch-sampler collage to try out different designs, movements, and thread-pattern flows.

« *My Dragonflies.* 9½" × 7" (24 × 18 cm); dye color, acrylic paint; free-motion stitching, hand embroidery.

» *Funflowers.* 12½" × 9" (31.5 × 23 cm); dye color; hand embroidery.

You Will Need

- Cotton, linen, or muslin fabric
- Embroidery hoop
- Embroidery threads and floss
- Chenille needles

The Process

1 Secure a piece of cotton, linen, or muslin fabric in an embroidery hoop. It should be taut like a drum.

2 Just stitch! No patterns are needed. Using basic embroidery stitches (see page 138), just keep adding stitches next to, around, and tucked inside each other until your whole fabric surface is covered *(Figure 1)*. The finished piece becomes an organic, moving example of thread play at its finest.

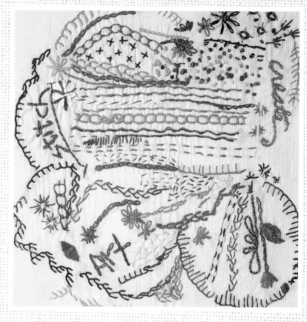

FIGURE 1

{TIP}

I always use a #18 or #22 chenille needle for handstitching because it is a larger needle and has a sharper point.

Keep Stitching

✳ Make a large doodle-stitched fabric piece for the central focal point of an art quilt.

✳ Put doodle-stitched fabric pieces in frames or embroidery hoops to use as decorative wall art.

✳ Choose a specific color story with your threads, then embroider pieces to match home décor or fabrics and use for decorative pillow covers.

DOODLE STITCH
journal

Materials

- 8" × 13¾" (20.5 × 35 cm) piece of muslin or linen for main cover fabric
- Thread
- Assorted pearl cottons and embroidery floss
- One fat quarter cotton fabric for border (I used batik fabric for border, lining, and binding)
- Fusible batting
- 15¼" × 9½" (38.5 × 24 cm) piece of fabric for lining
- ¼ yard (23 cm) piece of cotton fabric for binding
- Five 8½" × 12" (21.5 × 30.5 cm) sheets of watercolor or sketchbook paper
- Waxed linen thread
- Decorative button

Tools

- 5" (12.5 cm) embroidery hoop
- Chenille or embroidery needles
- Awl
- Tapestry needle

Finished Size

- About 7½" × 9¼" (19 × 23.5 cm) (closed)

Cozy up with a cup of tea and stitch to your heart's content. With no specific pattern or design in mind, just practice all your stitches and create colorful organic lines and shapes. Once you've turned your sampler into a centerpiece for the cover of a custom-made journal, you'll be inspired every time you pick it up.

Make the Cover

1   Zigzag stitch around the 8" × 13¾" (20.5 × 35 cm) piece of muslin or linen, about ¼" from the edges of the fabric, to prevent fraying. Place the fabric in an embroidery hoop.

2   Just stitch! Make continuous random lines of stitching in different colors and thread thicknesses to cover the entire surface from side to side and top to bottom. Don't worry about the labyrinth of threads on the back; it will be covered with batting and a lining. Press.

3   Cut pieces of fabric for the border: two 2" × 9¼" (5 × 23.5 cm) pieces and two 2" × 12" (5 × 30.5 cm) pieces.

4   Trim panel to 12" × 6¼" (30.5 × 16 cm).

5   Add the border (see page 132).

6   Work a frame of hand backstitch ⅜" (1 cm) outside center panel.

7   Fuse a piece of same-size batting onto the back of your stitched piece.

8   Wrong sides together, place stitched piece to lining. Pin. Piece should measure 15" × 9¼" (38 × 23.5 cm). Stitch around the edges of the piece with a ¼" (6 mm) seam allowance, leaving a 3" (7.5 cm) opening.

9   Turn the piece inside out and handsew the opening closed.

10 Add a binding (see page 132).

Assemble the Book

11 Fold your five sheets of 8½" × 12" (21.5 × 30.5 cm) paper in half widthwise and place in the fold of the stitched cover. With the awl, push three small holes through the paper and fabric: one in the center and one 2" (5 cm) above and below the center hole (*Figure 1*).

12 With the waxed linen on the tapestry needle, thread through the inside center, leaving a 2" (5 cm) tail. Go up to the top hole, come back into the fold and go down all the way across to the bottom hole and pull to the outside. Go back into the middle hole, coming into the center (*Figure 2*).

13 Gently pull the thread taut and tie the ends together.

14 Add a decorative button to the front cover. If you like, you can add a cord or ribbon to the back to create a closure.

» *Use a good-quality watercolor paper for the pages of your journal so it stands up to all of your creative sketching and doodling.*

» ***Assembly Diagram***

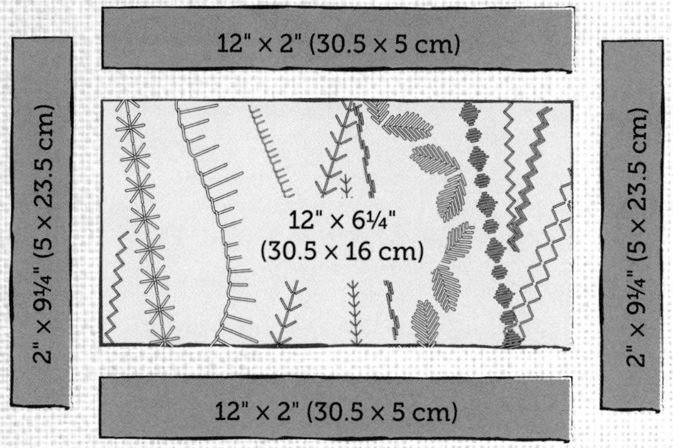

12" × 2" (30.5 × 5 cm)
2" × 9¼" (5 × 23.5 cm)
12" × 6¼" (30.5 × 16 cm)
2" × 9¼" (5 × 23.5 cm)
12" × 2" (30.5 × 5 cm)

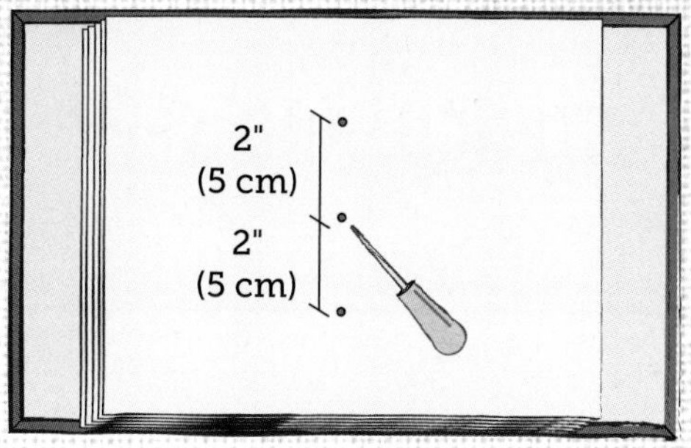

2" (5 cm)
2" (5 cm)

FIGURE 1

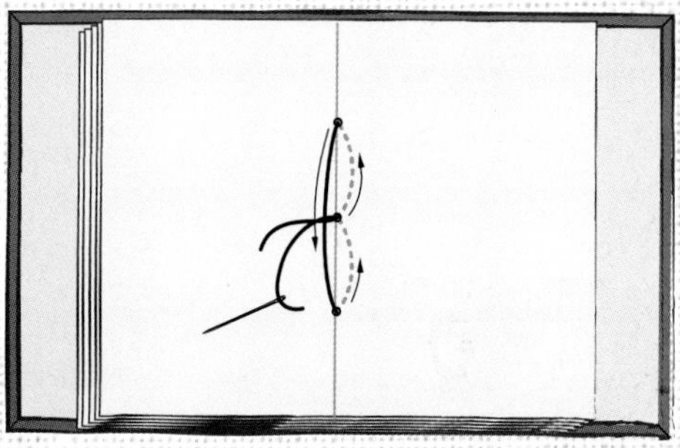

FIGURE 2

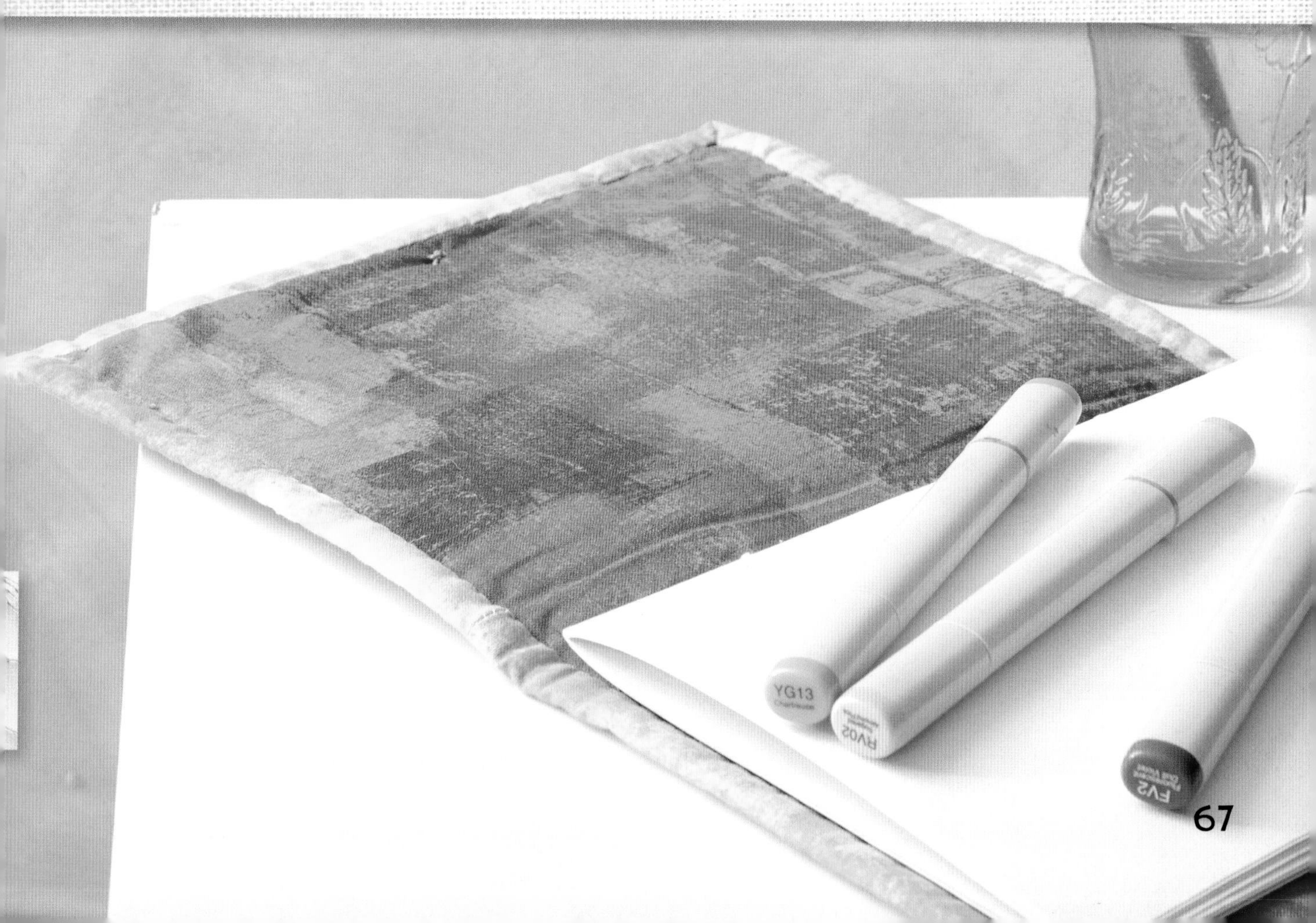

YG13
RV02
FV2

STENCIL AND SEW

Stencils can create instant imagery and patterns for stitchable art. And if you're a mixed-media artist, you might already have a lot of stencils!

Choose stencils with large cutouts, rather than tiny, intricate spaces. Daub paint on with a sponge or use spray-bottled fabric dyes to quickly cover your fabric surface in repeating allover patterns. Then enhance those patterns with machine or handstitching.

You Will Need

- Stencils
- Fabric paint or spray dyes
- Natural-colored muslin
- Glue stick
- Cosmetic sponges
- Sewing machine with darning foot and machine-sewing thread *or* chenille needles and embroidery floss and threads

» *Winged Hearts.* 9" × 9¾" (23 × 25 cm); dye color; handstitching, decorative machine stitching.

The Process

1   Gather a few of your favorite stencils *(Figure 1),* fabric paints, and pieces of natural-colored muslin to use as foundation pieces.

2   With a glue stick, lightly apply a small amount of glue to the back of the stencil (it will rinse off), so it won't move when placed on fabric. Place stencil onto fabric.

3   Use a cosmetic sponge to lightly dab the paint onto the stenciled image *(Figure 2).* If desired, lift the stencil, reposition it, and repeat pattern.

4   Enhance the designs with loose, free-motion stitching (see page 42) that outlines the shapes of the stenciled images *(Figure 3).*

FIGURE 1

FIGURE 2

Keep Stitching

✳ For more texture, hand embroider areas of the stenciled art with pearl cotton or floss.

✳ Make your own stencils by cutting designs out of thin cardboard with a craft knife.

✳ Lay found objects such as keys and leaves on fabric and spray with fabric dye to create a reverse stencil effect.

FIGURE 3

PEN AND BRUSH
tied roll

Materials
- 14" × 24" (35.5 × 61 cm) piece of muslin for outside of roll
- Fabric paint or acrylic paint with textile medium
- 14" × 14" (35.5 × 35.5 cm) piece of fusible batting
- 14" × 14" (35.5 × 35.5 cm) piece of fabric for lining
- Thread
- 2¼" × 24" (5.5 × 61 cm) piece of cotton fabric for tie

Tools
- Stencils
- Cosmetic sponges
- Tailor's chalk

Finished Size
- 13" × 13¾" (33 × 32 cm) (unrolled)

What better way to exhibit your art—and be ever-ready to make more—than to carry your pens and brushes in a handmade roll-up pouch? You can customize this storage with individual compartments to hold assorted sizes of brushes, pens, and pencils. You can even change the size of the roll to fit taller or shorter items, such as knitting needles or crochet hooks.

Stencil the Fabric

1 Cut two pieces of muslin fabric: one 14" × 14" (35.5 × 35.5 cm) and one 10" × 14" (25.5 × 35.5 cm).

2 With fabric paint (or acrylic paint with textile medium) and a cosmetic sponge, gently stencil a design onto the two pieces of fabric. Let the fabric dry completely.

Make the Roll

3 Apply lightweight fusible batting to batik lining piece. Place 14" × 14" (35.5 × 35.5 cm) stenciled piece to lining, right sides together. Sew around three sides with a ½" (1.3 cm) seam allowance, leaving the bottom edge unsewn. Turn right side out and press.

4 Fold 10" × 14" (25.5 × 35.5 cm) stenciled piece in half lengthwise, wrong sides together, to create pocket piece. Topstitch ⅜" (1 cm) from fold. Position pocket piece on the stenciled side of main roll piece, with raw edges aligned.

5 Stitch from the fold of the pocket down its side, across the bottom, and up the remaining side to the fold, using ⅜" (1 cm) seam allowance *(Figure 1)*.

6 Clip corners and fold pocket piece to lining side. This will cause side edges of roll above pocket to turn in ⅜" (1 cm). Press and machine-stitch ⅛" (3 mm) in from turned-back edge down sides and through the pocket *(Figure 2)*.
Note: Stitching will be visible on both sides, so use the same thread in machine and bobbin.

7 To create a fabric tie, fold the 2¼" × 24" (6.5 × 61 cm) piece of fabric in half lengthwise, with right sides together. Sew along the long edge and one short edge with a ¼" (6 mm) seam. Turn the piece right side out and tuck raw edges of opening inside. Press and stitch closed.

8 Measure roughly 1¾" (4.5 cm) vertical spaces on the inner pouch and mark with chalk. Sew straight lines from the bottom to the top to create seven compartments *(Figure 3)*. At the same time that you sew one of the lines near the center, sew the fabric tie to the back *(Figure 4)*.

9 Sew a horizontal line across the width of the piece where the top flap folds down *(Figure 5)*.

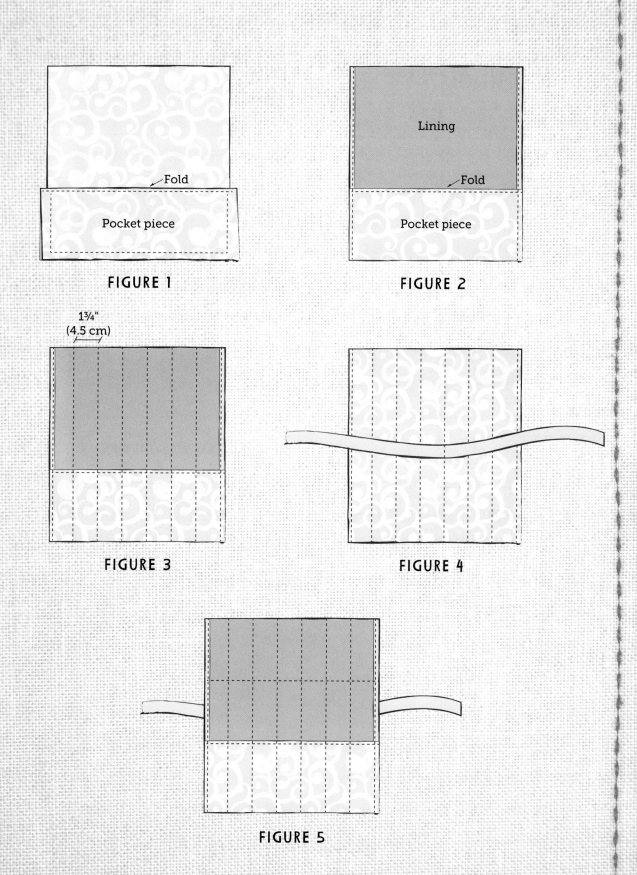

Fold

Pocket piece

FIGURE 1

Lining

Fold

Pocket piece

FIGURE 2

1¾"
(4.5 cm)

FIGURE 3

FIGURE 4

FIGURE 5

ARTFUL ALPHABETS APPLIQUÉ

Who needs a pattern to copy when you can use your own handwriting? I have devised a simple method to make appliqué letters that maintain the artist's distinct, recognizable style. With this technique, you can make whole alphabets and have individual letters handy for other future projects.

You can use the same transfer and fusing techniques to create appliqués of images from your own drawings. Combine words and images for a truly unique personal effect.

You Will Need

- Pencil and paper
- Black Sharpie marker
- Freezer paper
- Lightbox or other light source (optional)
- Assorted cotton fabrics for letters and background
- Fusible web
- Iron
- Sewing machine and machine-sewing thread

The Process

1 With a pencil, write out words or phrases on plain paper in your own writing (Figure 1).

2 Trace around the letters, exaggerating and changing the shapes of the letters (Figure 2).

3 Trace the letters with a black Sharpie marker onto the paper side of freezer paper (Figure 3). Use a lightbox or other light source (such as a window) to make it easier to see through the freezer paper.

4 Choose fabric for the letters and fuse the back side with fusible web.

5 Cut out the freezer paper letters (Figure 4), arrange them on the fabric background waxy side down, and iron down securely.

6 Cut out the letters and arrange them onto a fabric background and iron down securely.

7 Sew around the shape of each piece with straight, zigzag, or blanket stitches on your machine (Figure 5).

Keep Stitching

✳ What could be more special than an heirloom quilt with a child's name or initials in your personal lettering? Check the fusible-web manufacturer's instructions to make sure it can be laundered.

✳ Make freeform lettering by cutting out your fused pieces without a pattern.

✳ Appliqué around your letters and shapes with other decorative stitches on your sewing machine.

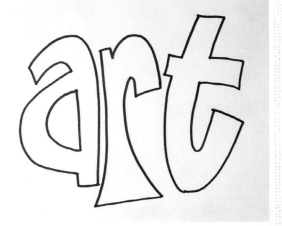

FIGURE 1

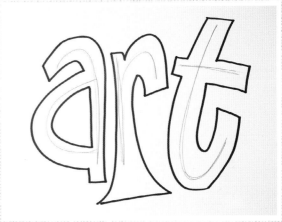

FIGURE 2

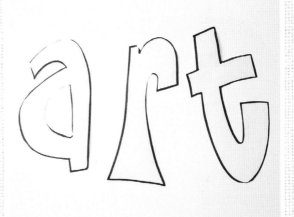

FIGURE 3

FIGURE 4

FIGURE 5

Fused Fabric Appliqué

In my art quilts and textile art, I use the rather unfussy technique of *raw-edge appliqué*, which involves sewing around appliqué shapes with straight, zigzag, or decorative machine stitches, without turning the edges under.

The product that enables you to do this is called *fusible web*. Fusible web is a fine glue sheet that is heat-set to fuse fabrics together. I have two preferred fusible-web products. Mistyfuse is a very lightweight webbing that is applied onto fabric and has no paper backing. You cut it to size and position it on the back of fabric, then place it in between a very sheer silicone "Goddess sheet" and heat-set with a dry iron.

The other product is a quilter's favorite called Lite Steam-A-Seam 2, a double-sided adhesive. This product has grid lines for cutting and a paper backing with a light adhesive to stick to fabric as you fuse and cut.

You will find your own favorite products for this technique. Just be sure to follow the manufacturer's directions on the packaging.

When you set the fusible web with an iron, use a pressing motion. Do not move the iron back and forth, which may shift or distort the design.

» **Love You Big.** *21½" × 20"*
(45.5 × 51 cm); fused appliqué.

» **Dream Big Little One.** *30" × 32"*
(76 × 81.5 cm); fused appliqué.

» **Be the Change.** 35" × 35" (89 × 89 cm); fused appliqué.

ART
makes
the
SOUL
visible

WHIMSICAL WORDS
art quilt

Materials
- Several fat quarters of fabric for appliqués
- Fusible web
- 30" x 40" (76 x 101.5 cm) piece of batik fabric for background
- ¼ yd (23 cm) batik fabric for border
- Cotton batting
- 1 yd (91.5 cm) fabric (44–45"/ 112–114.5 cm wide) for backing
- ¼ yd (23 cm) batik fabric for binding

Tools
- Sketchbook and colored pencils
- Iron
- Pencil
- Freezer paper
- Fine-tip permanent marker
- Sewing machine with darning foot

Finished Size
- About 33" × 43" (84 × 109 cm)

Make a bold statement with this colorful wall quilt. Choose a favorite quotation and an image to complement it. Using your own handwriting as a basis for the lettering guarantees your quilt will be literally one of a kind; just imagine the many wonderful custom gifts that can be created using this technique! You can use as few or as many colored fabrics for the appliqués as you like.

Appliqué the Quilt Top

1. Start by sketching your ideas for the finished quilt with colored pencils. Choose fabrics to coordinate with your sketch and apply fusible web to the backs of the fabric.

2. With a pencil, hand-letter the phrase "Art makes the soul visible" on the paper side of freezer paper. Still using the pencil, trace around the letters, changing and stretching the shape to create a stylized font.

3. Using a fine-tip Sharpie marker, trace around the new penciled shape on your freezer paper, making your own letter pattern design.

4. Cut out the words and arrange them on the right side of the pieces of fused fabric you're using for the lettering components, waxy side down.

5. Gently iron the freezer paper onto your fabric. Cut out your letters on the black outline of your patterns.

6. Repeat Steps 3 through 5 to make your pictorial elements for the quilt design.

7. Arrange your pieces onto your background fabric and fuse.

Assemble the Quilt

8. Cut pieces of fabric for border: Two pieces 1¾" × 40" (4.5 × 101.5 cm) and two pieces 1¾" × 32½" (4.5 × 82.5 cm). Sew the border (see page 132).

9. Add batting and a backing. Quilt the piece using free-motion stitching (see page 42), stitching around the appliqués and creating repetitive shapes such as leaves or pebbles.

10. Square off the quilt and add binding (see page 132).

« *Using multiple fabrics in your appliqués gives your piece even more color and texture.*

32½" × 1¾" (82.5 × 4.5 cm)

30" (76 cm)

40" × 1¾" (101.5 × 4.5 cm)

40" (101.5 cm)

40" × 1¾" (101.5 × 4.5 cm)

32½" × 1¾" (82.5 × 4.5 cm)

SKETCH AND STITCH

My stack of art journals provides me with many ideas and directions for making art to stitch. I especially enjoy lettering quotations and messages in my own handwriting and then stitching over them with colorful threads and floss.

Check out your own sketchbooks for ideas and letter your words on plain or printed fabric. When your own handwriting serves as the pattern for your handstitching, your pieces will exhibit your personality with a panache that can't be imitated.

{TIP}

I don't use pencil for this technique because I find it smears too much. I don't usually use a disappearing-ink pen either because sometimes if I have to put the project aside and am delayed in getting back to it, the ink fades and my drawing has disappeared!

» *Art Feeds Your Soul.* 11¼" × 13" (28.5 × 33 cm); hand embroidery. (See page 130 for a template.)

You Will Need

- Drawings or sketches (optional)
- Tracing paper or plain paper
- Pencil
- Colored markers (optional)
- Muslin
- Fine-tip permanent marker
- Embroidery hoop
- Embroidery threads and floss
- Chenille needles

The Process

1 Gather your favorite art doodles and drawings from your sketchbooks and journals and trace them onto tracing paper or draw a new image to stitch *(Figure 1)*.

2 If you want, you can color over the lines of your drawing with colored markers to figure out which colors of thread you'd like to use to stitch the image *(Figure 2)*.

3 With a fine-tip pigment pen such as a Pitt or Micron, trace your design onto muslin fabric *(Figure 3)*.

4 Place the fabric in an embroidery hoop and, using a variety of embroidery stitches (see page 138) outline the design in threads *(Figure 4)*. You can also fill in areas with satin and backstitches.

FIGURE 1

FIGURE 2

FIGURE 3

FIGURE 4

Project

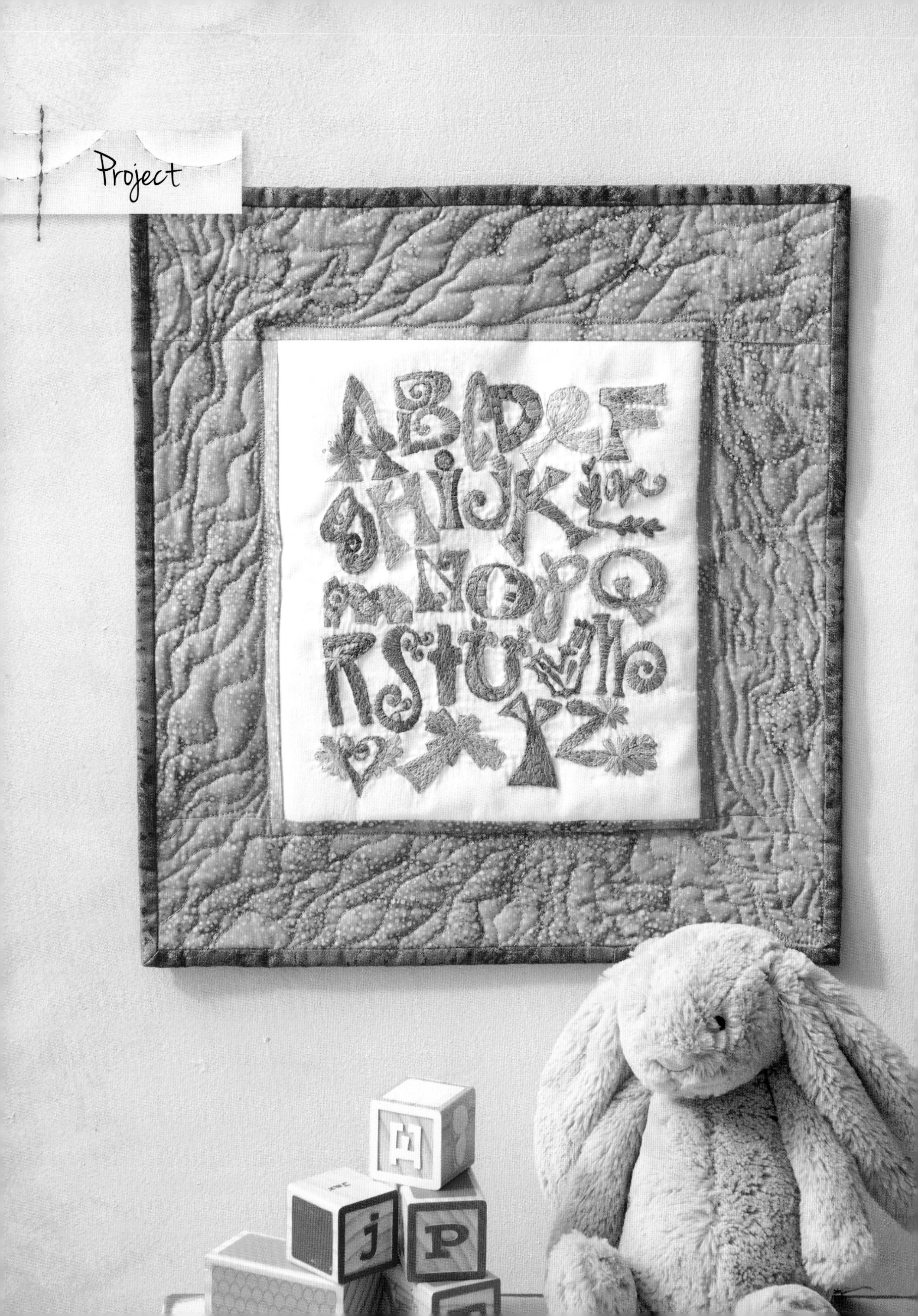

You Will Need

- Assorted embellishments
- Paints, fabric dyes, and markers
- Fabric
- Sewing machine
- Machine-sewing thread

The Process

1   Start a collection of interesting embellishments, such as doilies, lace, ribbons, threads, and scraps of fabric *(Figure 1)*. Antique and thrift shops, eBay, and Etsy are great hunting grounds for these items.

2   Dye, color, or paint the embellishments to transform them into new elements for art *(Figure 2)*.

3   Arrange and stitch these pieces onto a fabric base *(Figure 3)*. Use muslin you've painted or colored, printed fabrics, or even quilt blocks for maximum texture.

Keep Stitching

✳ Use heavily embellished decorative surfaces inspired by crazy quilting for totes and bags.

✳ Make gorgeous, decadent pillows for gifts and home décor in various sizes, large and small.

✳ In keeping with the traditional use of historic crazy quilts, craft over-the-top decorative quilts to display as fashion for your furniture.

FIGURE 1

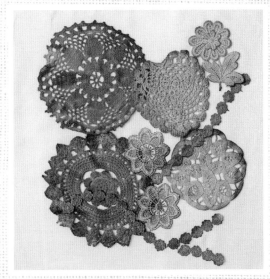

FIGURE 2

FIGURE 3

CRAZY PATCH
table runner

Materials

- Assorted fabrics for base quilt (plain cottons, hand-dyed fabrics, silks)
- Fusible featherweight interfacing
- Assorted pearl cottons and embroidery threads
- Assorted embellishments (lace, silk embroidery ribbons, rickrack, doilies)
- Cotton batting
- ½ yard (45.5 cm) cotton fabric for backing
- ¼ yard (23 cm) cotton fabric for binding

Tools

- Rotary cutter
- Iron
- Chenille or embroidery needles

Finished Size

- 11½" × 33½" (29 × 85 cm)

Think outside the quilt block to create this exuberant table runner. It's a larger surface on which you'll have plenty of room to add texture and color. This piece doesn't use traditional crazy-quilting techniques, but is inspired by the over-the-top stitching in which too much is perfectly just right. That's the beauty of being an artist—you take inspiration from something that speaks to your soul and move it in your own creative direction.

Make the Base Quilt

1   Make a 12" × 12" (30.5 × 30.5 cm) quilt block as follows: Cut a piece of fabric roughly in the shape of a crooked house with a pointed roof (about 6" × 6" [15 × 15 cm]) *(Figure 1)*.

2   Working in a counterclockwise direction and with right sides together, sew assorted-size strips of fabric to the center shape with a ¼" (6 mm) seam *(Figure 2)*. After you add each strip, fold it back and use a rotary cutter to trim the ends *(Figure 3)*.

3   Continue adding strips, maintaining the "house" shape at the center until block measures at least 13" (33 cm) at every point. Trim the piece into a 12" × 12" (30.5 × 30.5 cm) square *(Figures 4 and 5)*.

4   Repeat Steps 1 through 3 to create two more blocks.

5   Add fusible featherweight interfacing to the back of each block, then sew them into a strip with ½" (1.3 cm) seams.

Embellish and Finish the Runner

6   Embellish the runner top with embroidery stitches, ribbons, doilies, rickrack—whatever strikes your fiber fancy. This is a project that can take months as you create each tiny detail. Stitch and rest, stitch and rest. This is not a one-sitting project, but it's very portable. Tote it along with you in a small bag and indulge in some stitching bliss wherever you go.

7   When you're satisfied with the piece, add quilt batting and backing fabric. Bind the quilt (see page 132).

» *Explore crazy quilting and strip-piecing techniques to create the base for a playful, over-the-top embellished art piece.*

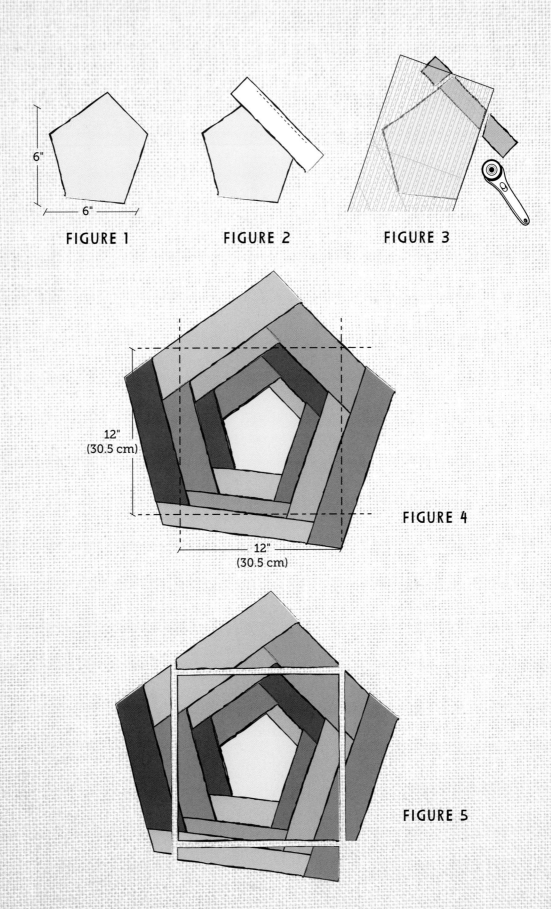

6"

6"

FIGURE 1

FIGURE 2

FIGURE 3

12"
(30.5 cm)

12"
(30.5 cm)

FIGURE 4

FIGURE 5

MIXED-MEDIA ART FABRIC

To "just paint" without a specific intention, design, image, or pattern is liberating. I love to make piles of painted muslin or colorful cottons that I can cut up and turn into mixed-media stitched collages. It seems that every painted piece ends up having a purpose in the grand scheme of making pictorial collages.

You can add texture using stamps, bubble wrap, cardboard, and myriad other found objects.

You Will Need

- Plain muslin
- Acrylic paints
- Inks
- Watercolor brush
- Found objects (bubble wrap, cardboard, etc.)
- Glue stick
- Sewing machine
- Machine-sewing thread

The Process

1 Cut several generously sized but manageable pieces of prewashed, pressed, plain muslin fabric to serve as your painting canvases. A 12" × 18" (30.5 × 45.5 cm) piece should work well. Gather assorted acrylic paints, inks, and brushes and just paint! Let loose and doodle with your paintbrush without any specific imagery in mind. Make abstract organic shapes, circles, lines, stripes, geometric shapes—anything you fancy. Use found objects like bubble wrap, corrugated cardboard, stamps, and stencils to add interest to the fabric patterns and color stories (Figure 1).

2 Cut the fabric into abstract shapes or elements for a collaged image (Figure 2).

3 Arrange the pieces on a piece of base fabric. You can use batiks, printed cottons, or muslin you've painted and colored. Use a glue stick to secure the shapes.

4 With a sewing machine, stitch around each piece using a zigzag or blanket stitch to secure (Figure 3).

{TIP}

Cover your work table with freezer paper (waxy side up) to use as the painting surface. Your fabric won't stick when the fibers are wet from the paint.

» Here's another example of making custom painted fabric using bubble wrap dipped as a stamp.

Keep Stitching

* Create an art quilt of faces or a self-portrait with colorful painted fabric pieces.
* Make an inspirational book in which each page is a collage of abstract imagery.
* Write and doodle on acrylic-painted scraps with a pigment marker, then paste into the pages of a sewn book.

FIGURE 1

FIGURE 2

FIGURE 3

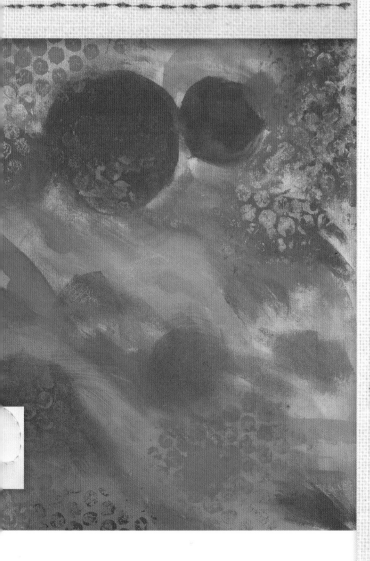

Project

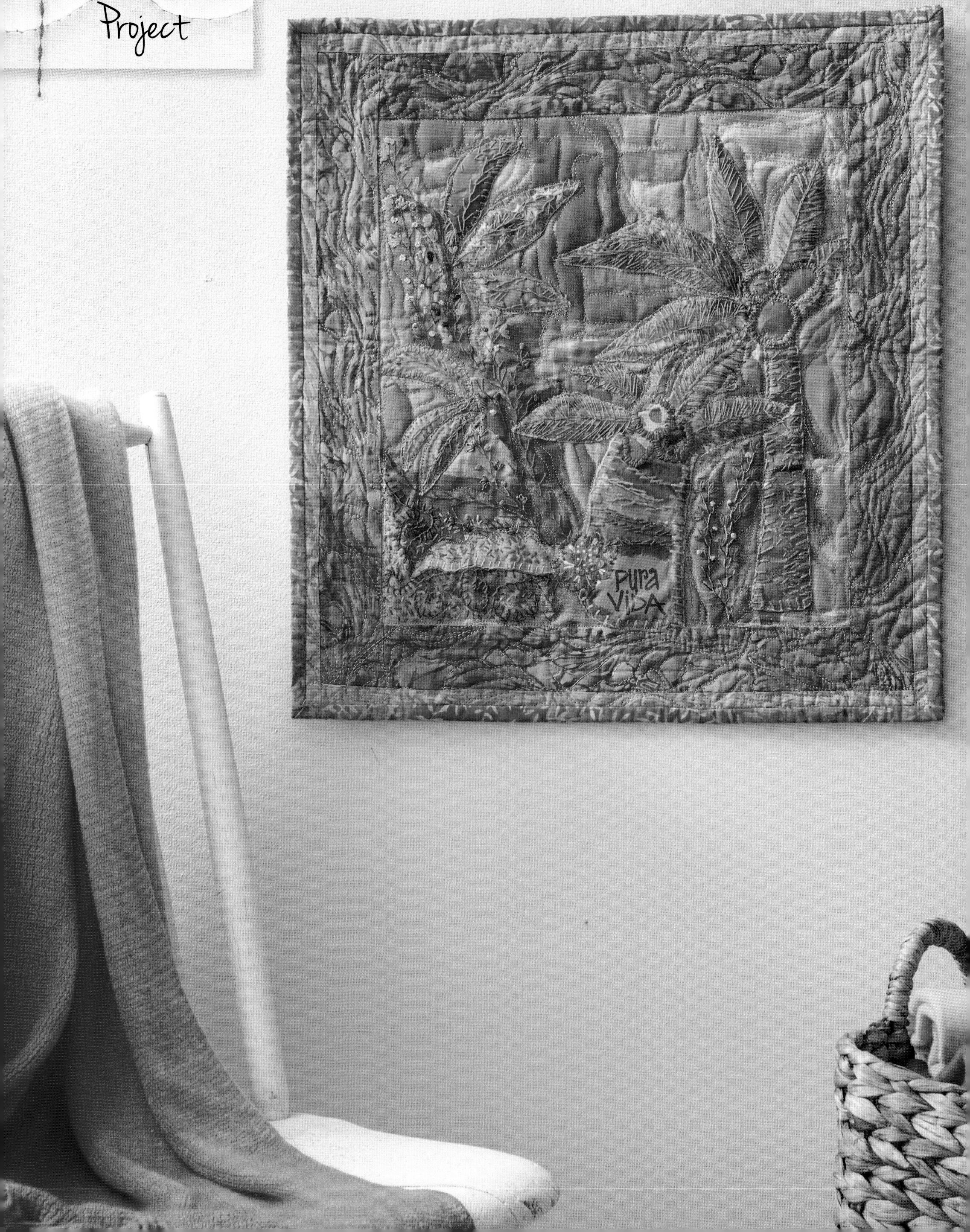

TRAVEL MEMORIES
story quilt

Materials

- Several 12" × 12" (30.5 × 30.5 cm) pieces of muslin for painting
- Fabric paint or acrylic paint with textile medium
- 12½" × 13½" (31.5 × 34.5 cm) piece of muslin for base
- Glue stick
- Assorted pearl cottons and embroidery floss
- Chenille or embroidery needles
- ½ yard (45.5 cm) of cotton fabric for inner border (I used batik for borders, backing, and binding)
- ¼ yard (23 cm) of cotton fabric for outer border
- Cotton batting
- ½ yard (45.5 cm) of cotton fabric for backing
- ¼ yard (23 cm) of cotton fabric for binding

Tools

- Sketchbook and pencil
- Paintbrush

Finished Size

- 17" × 18" (43 × 45.5 cm)

Make an art piece that tells a story and captures the colorful memories of a special trip. If you have travel sketches or photos, you can use them to brainstorm ideas for imagery and color inspiration for the painted fabrics you'll transform into an eye-catching wall quilt. This will become the very definition of a conversation piece!

Create the Central Image

1 With acrylics or fabric paints, loosely paint several 12" × 12" (30.5 × 30.5 cm) pieces of muslin. Remember, just paint! Make stripes, blocks of color, nature imagery, or anything you desire. Let the fabric dry completely.

2 While your paint dries, make a few sketches in a journal or sketchbook of possible compositions for your quilt. I used abstract palm trees to convey my memories of Costa Rica. Your image need not be realistic, but should evoke emotions and memories from the trip you're commemorating.

3 Cut up your painted fabrics, creating elements that resemble your sketch. Arrange the pieces and lightly secure to your base fabric with a glue stick.

4 Embellish the design with embroidery to add texture and to outline and define your design.

Make the Quilt

5 Cut pieces for borders of quilt:
Inside border: two 2¼" × 17" (5.5 × 43 cm) pieces; two 2¼" × 12½" (5.5 × 31.5 cm) pieces
Outside border: two 1" × 18" (2.5 × 45.5 cm) pieces; two 1" × 16" (2.5 × 40.5 cm) pieces

6 Sew the borders to the central piece (see page 132).

7 Square up your quilt top (page 132) to be 16¾" × 17¼" (42.5 × 44 cm). Add batting and quilt the piece. Add backing and bind the quilt (see page 132). Sew on a sleeve (see page 135), and it's ready to be displayed!

» *Use bold hand embroidery stitches to accentuate the painted fabric shapes that create the imagery.*

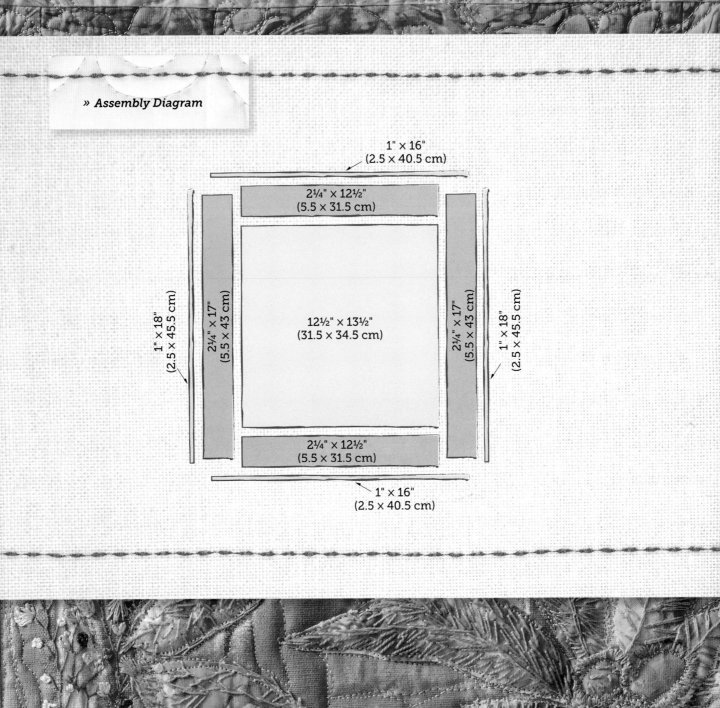

1" × 16"
(2.5 × 40.5 cm)

2¼" × 12½"
(5.5 × 31.5 cm)

1" × 18"
(2.5 × 45.5 cm)

2¼" × 17"
(5.5 × 43 cm)

12½" × 13½"
(31.5 × 34.5 cm)

2¼" × 17"
(5.5 × 43 cm)

1" × 18"
(2.5 × 45.5 cm)

2¼" × 12½"
(5.5 × 31.5 cm)

1" × 16"
(2.5 × 40.5 cm)

FABRIC STASH COLLAGE

I like to refer to this technique as fabric painting, with no paint required! Instead, you arrange fabric shapes backed with fusible web to create imagery, piling on bits of colorful fabric as if they were brushstrokes. Then you add repetitive stitching and echo the designs with layers of free-motion stitching.

I prefer to use batiks for this technique because they offer many, many colors and texture choices that readily translate into imagery. But you could use solids or prints to achieve other interesting results.

» *Whimsy Garden.* *13½" × 10" (34.5 × 25.5 cm); fused appliqué, hand embroidery, free-motion stitching.*

You Will Need

- Sketching materials
- Batiks and other printed fabrics
- Fusible web
- Iron
- Sewing machine with darning foot
- Machine-sewing thread

The Process

1 Sketch out a design for your collage. Gather colorful batik and printed fabrics that will work for your sketch.

2 Apply fusible web to the backs of the pieces you will use in the collage.

3 Free-hand cut out your design elements (Figure 1).

4 Referring to your sketch, arrange the pieces on your foundation fabric (Figure 2).

5 Iron over the front side of the pieces to secure them to the foundation fabric.

6 Use machine stitching and colorful threads to enhance the design, creating line and movement (Figure 3).

{TIP}

Add hand-embroidery stitches for even more texture and interest.

FIGURE 1

FIGURE 2

FIGURE 3

» *Spirit.* 10" × 10" (25.5 × 25.5 cm); fused appliqué.

» *Work in Progress.* 12¼" x 10" (31 x 25.5 cm); fused appliqué.

» *Fly.* 12" x 12" (30.5 × 30.5 cm); fused appliqué.

Keep Stitching

✳ Make a travel journal with a collage cover that illustrates the theme of the journey.

✳ Use your own stash of colorful dyed, or painted fabric scraps to make the collage imagery.

BUTTERFLIES
book cover

Materials

- Eight to ten 12" × 12" (30.5 × 30.5 cm) pieces of cotton fabric
- Fusible web
- 15" × 20" (38 × 51 cm) piece of muslin fabric for base (for a standard 8" × 11" [20.5 × 28 cm] composition book; or 2" [5 cm] larger on all sides than the book you're covering)
- 15" × 20" (38 × 51 cm) piece of cotton quilt batting
- 15" × 20" (38 × 51 cm) piece of fabric for lining
- Thread
- 11" × 12" (28 × 30.5 cm) piece of fabric for inside flaps
- Composition book

Tools

- Iron
- Sewing machine with darning foot

Finished Size

- 8" × 11" (20.5 × 28 cm) (closed)

Remember the schoolbook covers children used to make out of brown paper grocery bags? This composition book cover is a much more colorful, personalized version of the same thing. Create whimsical imagery from assorted printed fabrics. I have allowed the design to flow from the front to the back of my book cover, but there are, of course, as many ways to compose this project as there are artists.

Make the Collage Fabric

1 Iron fusible web to your 12" × 12" (30.5 × 30.5 cm) pieces of fabric.

2 Cut several fabric squares into random shapes of different sizes from about 4½– 13" (11.5–33 cm) long and up to about 2½" (6.5 cm) wide. These will cover the base of your book cover.

3 Cut your base fabric 2" (5 cm) larger on all sides than the book you'll be covering.

4 Lay the pieces you cut in Step 2 on top of the base piece and fuse *(Figure 1)*. Trim any pieces that go beyond the edges of the base fabric.

5 To make the butterflies, cut out many different-size heart shapes; these will be the heads and wings. Cut several skinny ovals for the butterflies' bodies.

6 Arrange the pieces on the base fabric so the butterflies are scattered in a pleasing composition. Fuse the butterflies to the background *(Figure 2)*.

 {TIP}

I have a bin that's always filled with assorted fabrics fused and ready to go into projects.

Make the Book Cover

7 Make a quilt sandwich with the fused top, the cotton batting, and the lining fabric. Stitch over the entire design with free-motion sewing. Loosely "draw" with thread to outline the butterflies and give them details *(Figure 3)*.

8 Trim the quilted fabric to 2" (5 cm) larger than the opened composition book.

9 Cut two pieces of fabric 12" × 11" (30.5 × 28 cm; or depth of cover) for each inside pocket of the cover, which will secure the composition book in place. If your book is a different size, cut the pieces to the height of your book by twice the depth you'd like your pockets to be.

10 Fold pocket pieces in half lengthwise, wrong sides together, and press to create two 6" × 11" (15 × 28 cm) pockets. Turn cover to inside/lining side and position 11" (28 cm) raw edges of pocket pieces flush with 11" (28 cm) sides of cover. Pin to secure *(Figure 4)*.

11 Zigzag-stitch around the edge of the entire cover, attaching smaller interior pieces in the stitching line *(Figure 5)*. Insert cover of composition book into pockets and fold in half to close.

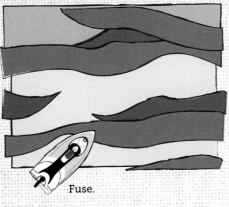

FIGURE 1

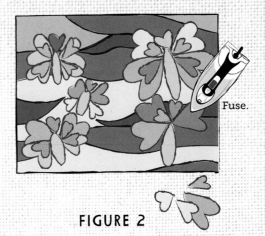

FIGURE 2

Batting   Lining

FIGURE 3

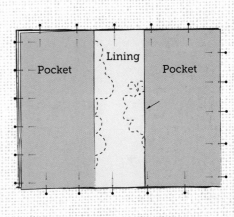

Pocket   Lining   Pocket

FIGURE 4

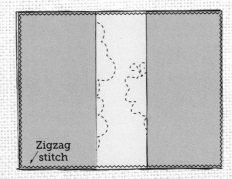

Zigzag
stitch

FIGURE 5

SCRAPPY SNIPS COLLAGE CLOTH

Once you start making art with fabrics, you'll find that you accumulate the most delicious piles of gorgeous scraps and snippets. If you upcycle these pieces to create new fabric for your projects, their potential explodes.

Arrange colorful scraps into sheets, then add quilting lines to secure the pieces and create movement. You can use straight or curvy lines, or a combination.

Try out a more abstract and geometric approach with this technique, which focuses on the spatial relationships of colorful fabrics.

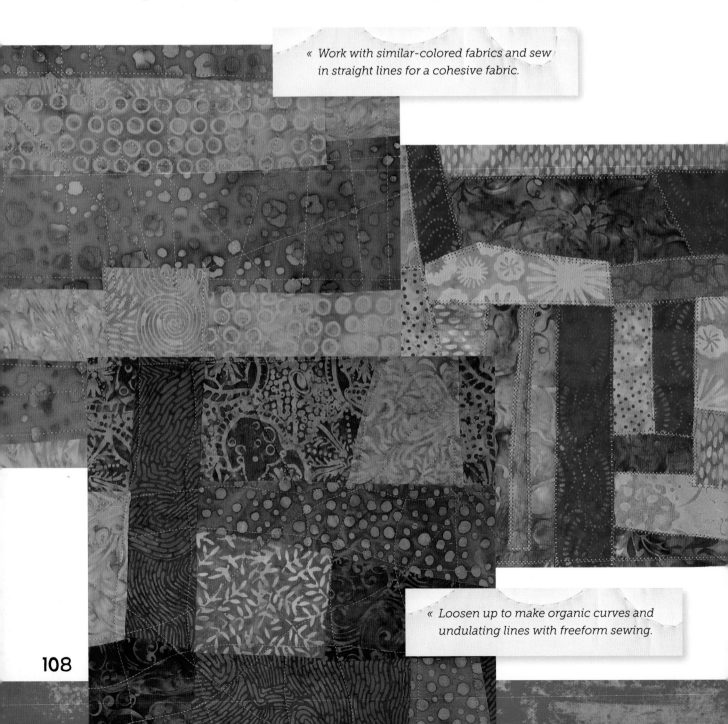

« Work with similar-colored fabrics and sew in straight lines for a cohesive fabric.

« Loosen up to make organic curves and undulating lines with freeform sewing.

You Will Need

- Batik or other printed fabric
- Scissors
- Fusible web
- Iron
- Muslin
- Cotton batting
- Sewing machine
- Thread

The Process

1 Cut up batik or other printed fabrics into wide and narrow strips *(Figure 1)*.

2 Apply fusible web to a piece of muslin fabric to use as a base. Build a geometric composition with the strips of fabric. Press and secure the pieces to the base fabric *(Figure 2)*.

3 Make a quilt sandwich with the scrappy piece as the top, batting in the middle, and a liner fabric on the bottom. Use one color of contrasting thread and quilt with straight and zigzag stitches, covering the entire surface, side to side and top to bottom *(Figure 3)*.

4 Cut the fabric into desired sizes and shapes for projects.

« *Cut out wonky geometric shapes and showcase each piece as patchwork with a machine blanket stitch. Use a single color or metallic thread to embellish and highlight the edges of each shape.*

FIGURE 1

FIGURE 2

FIGURE 3

PATCHYWORK
peeper keeper

Materials

- 7" × 8" (18 × 20.5 cm) or larger piece of muslin for base
- Fusible web
- Assorted cotton fabric scraps in your favorite colors
- 7" × 8" (18 × 20.5 cm) piece of lightweight interfacing
- 7" × 8" (18 × 20.5 cm) piece of cotton fabric for lining
- Contrasting color thread
- 3" × 6" (7.5 × 15 cm) piece of contrasting cotton fabric for top band

Tools

- Iron

Finished Size

- 2¾" × 6¾" (7 × 17 cm)

It's so easy to create this narrow little pouch from your handmade collage cloth. Contrasting trim makes it chic and eye-catching, and the quilted fabric will amply protect your specs. Whip one up for every pair of glasses, readers, and sunglasses you own. Pop in your peepers and you're good to go!

Make the Collage Fabric

1   Iron fusible web onto a 7" x 8" (18 x 20.5 cm) piece of muslin. This will be the base for your collage fabric.

2   Cut your fabric scraps into small, wonky geometric shapes and arrange them on top of the fusible web in a random yet pleasing pattern. Press the fabric to fuse. Trim any pieces that go beyond the edges of the base fabric.

3   When the pieces are in place, make a "sandwich" in this order: the top collaged piece, lightweight interfacing, and lining fabric.

4   With a contrasting color thread, quilt the scrappy fabric with basic straight and zigzag stitches in straight and curving lines. Run the stitches over the edges of the scraps to secure the shapes.

Construct the Pouch

5   Cut a piece of your collage fabric to 6" x 7" (15 x 18 cm).

6   Fold the piece of contrasting cotton fabric for the top band in half lengthwise, wrong sides together, and press, creating a 1½" x 6" (3.8 x 15 cm) piece. Align raw edges of band to top (6"/15 cm) wrong (lining) side of collage fabric piece. Stitch across ¼" (6 mm) from edge *(Figure 1)*.

7   Fold band to right side, press and top-stitch with contrast thread ⅛" (3 mm) from lower fold *(Figure 2)*.

8   Fold the collage fabric in half lengthwise with the front to the inside and sew up the bottom and side with a ¼" (6 mm) seam *(Figure 3)*.

9   Turn the pouch inside out and push out the corners.

{TIP}

Make the pouch taller, shorter, or wider to use for paintbrushes, pens, hairstyling irons, or other delicate objects that could use cushioned storage.

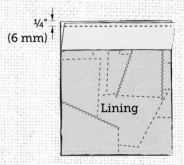

¼"
(6 mm)

Lining

FIGURE 1

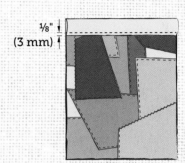

⅛"
(3 mm)

FIGURE 2

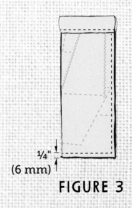

¼"
(6 mm)

FIGURE 3

WHIMSICAL WOOLS

In most of the techniques in this book, we work with fabric, but here's a chance to try your hand at basic needlefelting and wool appliqué. Needlefelting is the process of taking wool roving and condensing it into fabric using a special barbed needle or tool with multiple needles. You can combine various colors to create abstract patterns or recognizable motifs.

But of course you don't have to stop there. You can then embellish the piece with wool felt, textured yarns, threads, fabric scraps, beads, and more. Work with the couching stitch (see page 139) to attach thick strands of yarns and roving. Cut out wool shapes from hand-dyed felt and add on to the pieces with decorative handstitching. Just pile it on!

You Will Need

- Wool roving, felt pieces, yarns, embroidery threads, fabric pieces, lace
- Wool felt
- Felting tool or felting needles
- Chenille needles

The Process

1 Gather an assortment of wool roving, felt pieces, textured yarns, embroidery threads, embellishment fabrics, and lace and arrange them loosely on a sheet of wool felt (Figure 1).

2 Gently pounce the wool roving and fibers into the base sheet of wool felt with a commercial felting tool or individual felting needles. Be very careful handling these needles; they are very, very sharp! Build layers with assorted colors and textures until the desired result is achieved (Figure 2).

3 Add accents and handstitching with embroidery threads and yarns (Figure 3).

» **Felted Fantasy.** 12" × 9" (30.5 × 23 cm); needlefelting; hand embroidery.

Keep Stitching

✳ Create a stitching sampler book to try out a wide variety of threads, floss, yarns, ribbons, and fabrics.

✳ Assemble richly textured art quilts with layers of layers of felted fibers. You can also add vintage embellishments and decorative metal charms and trinkets.

✳ Design mini art quilts with handstitched wool appliqué shapes that tell a story.

✳ With fibers, wool shapes, roving, handstitching, and machine stitching, illustrate a colorful landscape or imaginary place.

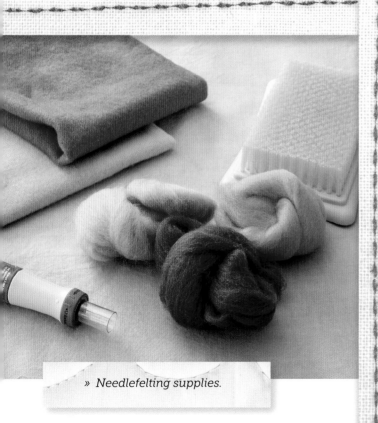

» Needlefelting supplies.

FIGURE 1

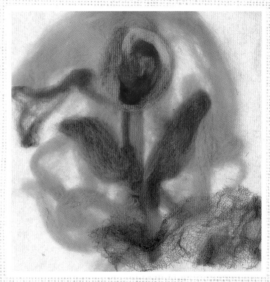

FIGURE 2

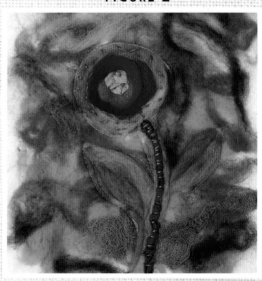

FIGURE 3

WONDERFULLY WOOLLY
needle book

Materials

- 7" × 11" (18 × 28 cm) piece of wool felt for fabric base
- Assorted bits of wool roving
- Textured yarns and fibers
- Scraps of wool felt
- Various colors of pearl cotton or embroidery floss
- 6" × 10½" (15 × 26.5 cm) piece of cotton fabric for lining
- 6" × 10½" (15 × 26.5 cm) piece of lightweight interfacing
- Two 5½" × 9½" (14 × 24 cm) pieces of wool felt for interior pages
- Button and ribbon for closure (optional)

Tools

- Thick needlefelting foam or needlefelting mat
- Handfelting tool or barbed felting needles
- Chenille or embroidery needles
- 90/14 quilting needle

Finished Size

- About 5½" × 7" (14 × 18 cm) (closed)

Take your stitching on the go with this easy-to-make "book" that stores your assorted needles, threaders, and pre-strung needles. You could easily sew a button on the front cover and a loop of ribbon on the back to create a closure. Include as many wool felt pages as you need to stash and grab all of your notions.

Make the Cover

1 Place a 7" × 11" (18 × 28 cm) piece of wool felt on felting foam or mat. This will be the cover of the needle book.

2 With the felting tool or barbed felting needles, carefully and rhythmically pounce assorted fibers and bits of roving into the wool felt. Build up layers and colors as you make organic shapes, lines, or simple images.

3 Embellish the front cover with cut-out wool shapes and embroidery stitches.

In my sample, I blanket-stitched a rectangular piece of felt to the front and layered wool circles for flowers. I finished with hand-embroidered stitches, then free-motion-stitched stems and leaves in decorative green thread.

Add the Lining and Pages

4 Apply lightweight interfacing to your 6" × 10½" (15 × 26.5 cm) piece of lining fabric. Working blanket stitch, center and attach lining to inside of book *(Figure 1)*.

» *Use your own stitched art to create an innovative storage solution for your stitching tools!*

Do not worry whether the wool border is perfectly even around the edges.

5 For the interior pages, stack two 5½" × 9½" (14 × 24 cm) pieces of felt together and, using a sewing machine with a 90/14 quilting needle, sew them down the middle with a straight stitch, attaching them to the cover *(Figure 2)*.

6 Optional: Add a button to the front cover and a loop of ribbon to the back to create a closure.

{TIP}

If you're adding a closure ribbon, tuck its ends between the lining and the book cover before blanket-stitching in Step 4.

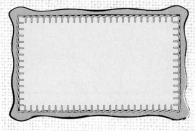

FIGURE 1

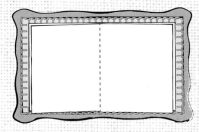

FIGURE 2

Start Simple

The Embellisher machine by Baby Lock is a valuable tool in my stitching studio. It's a motorized needle system that presses wool fibers into a base felt, creating new felted fabrics.

Before you invest big bucks in specialized machinery, however, try the process with more simple tools. See if it's a craft that you would like to grow with. As an introduction to needlefelting, start with the simple tools from the Clover company available at craft stores or online. They are safe, affordable, easy to find, and work great. You can always trade up to more sophisticated tools if you decide to seriously pursue needlefelting.

Home sweet Home

imagine
INSPIRE
CELEBRATE

Part 3

THE ARTFUL IMAGERY SKETCHBOOK

Many of the techniques in this book incorporate lettering and imagery. Here's where you might be saying, "But I can't draw!" You don't need to be able to draw well to create whimsical stitched art. Start with simple designs and shapes. Use the artwork and doodles from your own personal journals or copy these drawing ideas from my sketchbook pages to jumpstart your own artwork. You can grow and expand as you develop your own vision and combine your artwork and stitching to make signature works.

IMAGERY TRANSFER TIPS

In these pages, you'll find lots of drawings and words from my personal sketcbooks. Feel free to use them in your own stitched artwork.

You Will Need

- Patterns shown here or sketchbook of your own doodles and drawings
- Tracing paper or vellum and pencil (if using your own sketches)
- Photocopier (optional)
- Lightbox (or light source, such as a window) for tracing
- Fine-tip pigment pens
- Project fabrics

The Process

1 If you're using your own drawings, trace them with a pencil onto tracing paper or vellum.

2 Enlarge the drawings on a photocopier if needed for specific projects.

3 Using a lightbox for other light source to illuminate the drawings; trace them onto your project fabrics with a fine-tip pigment pen.

4 Use a light source to illuminate the drawing to transfer onto fabrics with a fine-tip pigment pen.

5 Hand or machine stitch, paint, or appliqué the images.

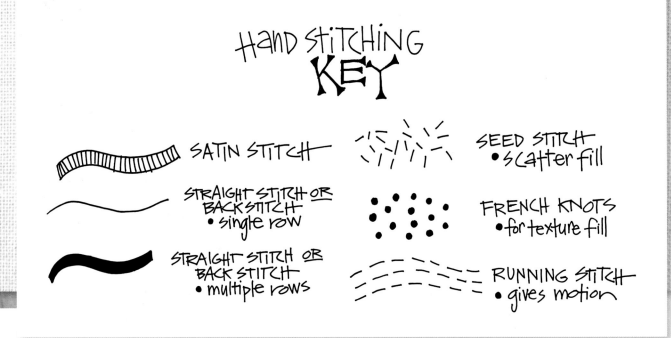

HAND STITCHING KEY

SATIN STITCH

STRAIGHT STITCH OR BACK STITCH • single row

STRAIGHT STITCH OR BACK STITCH • multiple rows

SEED STITCH • scatter fill

FRENCH KNOTS • for texture fill

RUNNING STITCH • gives motion

{TIP}

Start a sketchbook in an inexpensive composition book for your ideas and doodles. Use colored pencils to choose color stories and fabrics if needed.

the "onion flower"

{TIP}

Another way to transfer drawings to fabric is with Transdoodle by Mistyfuse. Place the Transdoodle paper with the chalky side down onto the fabric and place your drawing on top. Trace with a ballpoint pen to transfer the pattern. The chalklike transfer lines wipe off with a damp cloth.

whimsical
"winged things"
to stitch.

Fly

» Hearts

» Houses

Home sweet Home

HOME IS WHERE your story LIVES

» Teatime

{TIP}

Enlarge or reduce the images to use several in one project.

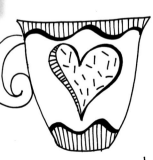

breathe

live in the MOMENT

Love you to the MOON and back.

Let your light SHINE

love LAUGH

joy

create

imagine

faith

inspire

BRAVE

CELEBRATE

just be.

{TIP}

Use colorful floss and thread to fill simple, basic shapes with line and pattern.

127

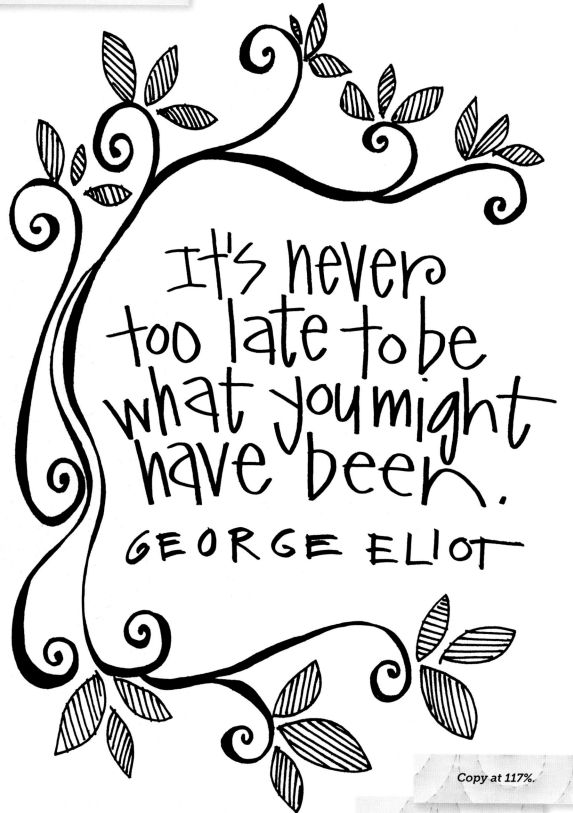

It's never too late to be what you might have been.

GEORGE ELIOT

Copy at 117%.

» Template for piece shown on page 12.

Copy at 133%.

» *This alphabet design is used in the Alphabet Baby Quilt project (page 84).*

» Use this template to stitch a design similar to the one shown on page 82.

Copy at 133%.

Art feeds your soul

» You can use this template for the Sketch and Stitch sample piece on page 83.

bloom

QUILTING AND SEWING BASICS

If you're new to sewing and quilting, or need a refresher, here are some techniques that will help with making the projects in this book.

Squaring Up

When you're creating a quilted project with a layer of batting in between the top and bottom layers, you need to make sure that all layers are flush around the edges before you finish the edges (usually by binding them).

Place your quilt onto a self-healing mat and square up the edges by using a metal yardstick or a rigid clear acrylic ruler and rotary cutter to trim each edge as necessary so that all layers are even and the corners form neat right angles. Use the edge of the ruler as a guide to make straight cuts with the rotary cutter *(Figure 1)*.

Sewing Borders

Many of my quilts feature a border around the central quilt design. Borders can have mitered corners (that meet at 45-degree angles), but I usually use simple squared corners. Here's how to add a simple squared border: Cut the border pieces to the sizes indicated in the project instructions. Depending on the quilt, either the top and bottom (horizontal)

border pieces or the side (vertical) border pieces will be the same width (or length) of the quilt. (Look at the assembly diagram if you're not sure.) Attach those pieces first by sewing them wrong side to wrong side with the quilt top using a ¼" (6 mm) seam. Press. Attach the remaining two pieces in the same way.

Binding

Cutting Straight Strips

Cut 2" (5 cm) strips on the crosswise grain, from selvedge to selvedge. Use a rotary cutter and straightedge ruler to obtain a straight cut. Remove the selvedges and join the strips with diagonal seams.

Cutting Bias Strips

Fold one cut end of the binding fabric to meet one selvedge, forming a fold at a 45-degree angle to the selvedge *(Figure 2)*. With the fabric placed on a self-healing mat, cut off the fold with a rotary cutter, using a straightedge ruler as a guide to make a straight cut. With the straightedge ruler and rotary cutter, cut 2" (5 cm) strips to the appro-priate width *(Figure 3)*. Join the strips with diagonal seams.

Diagonal Seams for Joining Strips

Lay two strips, right sides together, at right angles. The area where the strips overlap forms a square. Sew diagonally across the square. Trim the excess fabric ¼" (6 mm) away from the seam line *(Figure 4)* and press the seam allowances open. Repeat to join all the strips, forming one long fabric band.

Fold Binding

Option A: Double-Fold Binding This option will create binding that is similar to packaged double-fold bias tape/binding. Fold the strip in half lengthwise with wrong sides together; press. Open up the fold and then fold each long edge toward the wrong side, so that the raw edges meet in the middle *(Figure 5)*. Refold the binding along the existing center crease, enclosing the raw edges *(Figure 6)*, and press again.

Option B: Double-Layer Binding This option creates a double-thickness binding with only one fold. This binding is often favored by quilters. Fold the strip in half lengthwise with wrong sides together; press.

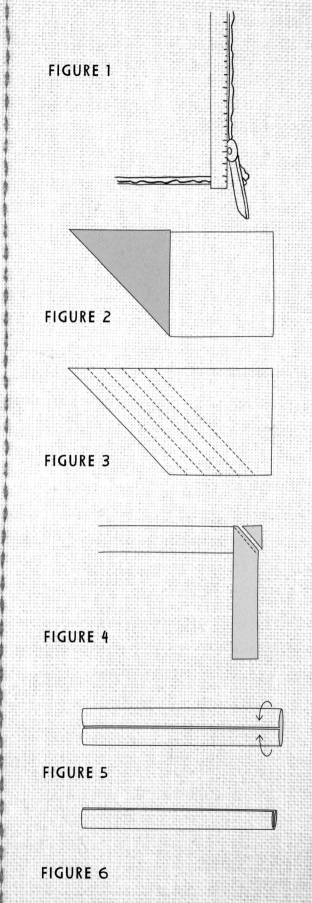

FIGURE 1

FIGURE 2

FIGURE 3

FIGURE 4

FIGURE 5

FIGURE 6

Binding with Mitered Corners

If using double-layer binding (option B), follow the alternate italicized instructions in parenthesis wherever you see them.

Open the binding and press ½" (1.3 cm) to the wrong side at one short end (refold the binding at the center crease and proceed). Starting with the folded-under end of the binding, place it near the center of the first edge of the project to be bound, matching the raw edges, and pin in place. Begin sewing near the center of one edge, along the first crease (at the appropriate distance from the raw edge), leaving several inches of the binding fabric free at the beginning. Stop sewing ¼" (6 mm) before reaching the corner, backtack, and cut the threads. Rotate the project 90 degrees to position it for sewing the next side. Fold the binding fabric up, away from the project, at a 45-degree angle *(Figure 1)*, and then fold it back down along the project raw edge *(Figure 2)*. This forms a miter at the corner. Stitch the second side, beginning at the project raw edge and ending ¼" (6 mm) from the next corner, as before. Continue as established until you have completed the last corner. Continue stitching until you are a few inches from the beginning edge of the binding fabric. Overlap the pressed beginning edge of the binding by ½" (1.3 cm, or overlap more as necessary for security) and trim the working edge to fit. Finish sewing the binding (opening the center fold and tucking the raw edge inside the pressed end of the binding strip). Refold the binding along all the creases and then fold it over the project raw edges to the back, enclosing the raw edges (there are no creases to worry about with option B). The folded edge of the binding strip should just cover the stitches visible on the project back. Slip-stitch the binding in place, tucking in the corners to complete the miters as you go *(Figure 3)*.

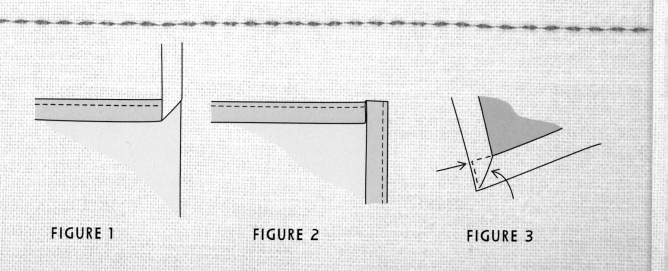

FIGURE 1　　　FIGURE 2　　　FIGURE 3

Making a Sleeve for Hanging Quilts

Cut a strip of plain muslin or backing fabric the width of the quilt and about 9" (23 cm) wide. Fold the short edges under ¼" (6mm) with wrong sides together. Fold the edges under again and press. Hem the folds with a straight or zigzag stitch. Fold the strip lengthwise with wrong sides together and sew the edges with a ½" (1.3 cm) seam allowance. Press the seam allowance open. Place the open seam against the quilt's back. Center and pin the top edge of the tube to the back of the quilt, about ½" (1.3 cm) below the binding. Whipstitch the top and bottom edges of the sleeve to the quilt backing. Whipstitch the back sides of the sleeve to the quilt.

Knots

Quilter's Knot (for handstitching)

1 Thread the needle and then grasp the eye of the needle with the thumb and forefinger of your nondominant hand. Bring the long end of the thread up so that the point of the needle and the end of the thread are facing each other and then slip the end of the thread between the fingers that are holding the eye of the needle (you now have a loop of thread hanging from the needle; *Figure 4*).

2 With your free hand, wrap the tail of the longer thread around the needle three times *(Figure 5)*.

3 Slide the wound thread down and lodge it between the fingers holding the eye of the needle and then, with your free hand, slowly pull the needle from the pointed end *(Figure 6)* until the entire length of thread has passed through your thumb and forefinger (still grasping the wound thread). The wound thread will form a small knot at the base of the thread.

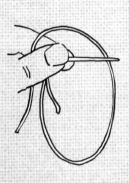

FIGURE 4

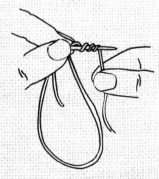

FIGURE 5

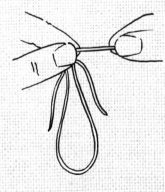

FIGURE 6

Finishing Knot (for handstitching)

Once you have completed your handstitching, you'll need to tie off your thread securely. I recommend using the following knot:

1   Insert your needle into the fabric where you would take your next stitch. Flip over the fabric so the wrong side is facing you and pull the thread completely through to the wrong side; hold the needle close to the fabric and wind the thread around the needle three times *(Figure 1)*.

2   Keeping the thread wound around the needle, insert the tip of the needle as close as possible to your last stitch *(Figure 2)*. Pivot the needle tip and bring it back through to the wrong side of the fabric, about ½" (1.3 cm) from where you inserted it. Pull the needle so that the working thread comes through the wound thread, forming a small knot *(Figure 3)*.

3   Give the thread a slight tug to pop the knot through the fabric. Cut the remaining thread with your embroidery scissors as close to the fabric as possible.

Square Knot

Working with two cords (or threads), make a loop from the right cord (pinch the cords together at the base of the loop between thumb and forefinger), and then thread the left cord through the loop from the bottom to top. Bring the left cord toward you and wrap it under and around the base of the right loop and then thread it through the loop from top to bottom *(Figure 4)*. Pull the cords tight.

Helpful Terms and Stitches

Bias

The direction across a fabric that is located at a 45-degree angle from the lenghwise or crosswise grain. The bias has high stretch and a very fluid drape.

Grain

The grain of a woven fabric is created by the threads that travel lengthwise and crosswise. The lengthwise grain runs parallel to the selvedges, the crosswise grain is perpendicular to the lenghwise threads.

Seam Allowance

The amount of fabric between the raw edge and the seam.

Selvedge

This is the tightly woven border on the lengthwise edges of woven fabric.

Slip Stitch

Working from right to left, join two pieces of fabric by taking a ¹⁄₁₆–¼" (2–6 mm) long stitch into the folded edge of one piece of fabric and bringing the needle out. Insert the needle into the folded edge of the other piece of fabric, directly across from the point where the thread emerged from the previous stitch. Repeat by inserting the needle into the first piece of fabric *(Figure 5)*. The thread will be almost entirely hidden inside the folds of the fabrics.

Topstitching

Topstitching is simply stitching that can be seen on the outside of a piece. It's used to hold pieces firmly in place and/or to add a decorative effect. To topstitch, make a line of stitching on the outside (right side) of the piece, usually a set distance from an existing seam.

Whipstitch

Bring the needle up at 1, insert at 2, and bring up at 3. Repeat (Figure 6). These quick stitches do not have to be very tight or close together.

FIGURE 1

FIGURE 2

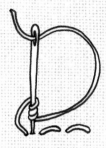

FIGURE 3

FIGURE 4

FIGURE 5

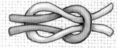

FIGURE 6

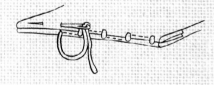

EMBROIDERY STITCHES

Pick and choose from the stitches shown here to artfully embellish your fabric and projects.

Backstitch

Working from right to left, bring the needle up at 1 and insert behind your starting point at 2. Bring the needle up at 3 (*Figure 1*). Repeat by inserting at 1 and then bring the needle up one stitch length beyond 3 (*Figure 2*).

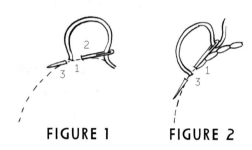

FIGURE 1   FIGURE 2

Blanket Stitch

Working from left to right, bring the needle up at 1 and insert at 2. Bring back up at 3 and over the working thread. Repeat. When using blanket stitch around the edge of an appliqué, be sure that the bottom of the stitches butt up against the edge of the appliqué.

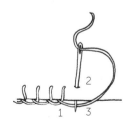

Chain Stitch

Working from top to bottom, bring the needle up at 1 and reinsert at 1 to create a loop; do not pull the thread taut. Bring the needle up at 2, through the loop, and gently pull the needle toward you to pull the loop flush with the fabric (*Figure 1*). Repeat by reinserting at 2 to create another loop and bring the needle up at 3 (*Figure 2*). To finish a row of stitches, tack down the last loop with a short running stitch.

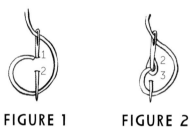

FIGURE 1   FIGURE 2

Chevron Stitch

Draw two parallel lines on the fabric with tailor's chalk. Starting at the lower line, take a small straight stitch to the right. Bring the needle back up at the center of the stitch (1). Insert the needle on the upper line at 2 and bring it up at 3 (*Figure 1*). Insert the needle at 4 and bring it back up at 2 (*Figure 2*). Work the stitches this way, alternately on the top and bottom lines (*Figures 3 and 4*).

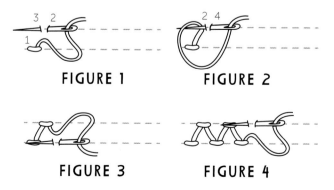

FIGURE 1   FIGURE 2

FIGURE 3   FIGURE 4

Couching Stitch

Working from right to left, use one thread, known as the couching, or working, thread, to tack down one or more laid threads or yarns (leave a tail of about 6" [15 cm] of the laid thread or yarn). Bring the working thread up at 1, insert at 2, and bring up at 3 (about ½" [1.3 cm] to the left of 2). When finished, leave a tail of about 6" (15 cm) on the laid thread or yarn and use a tapestry needle to bring it to the wrong side of the fabric, then tie off and trim. Repeat at the other end of the laid thread or yarn.

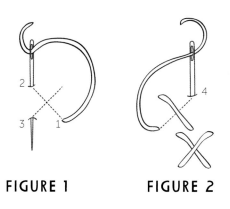

Cross-Stitch

Working from right to left, bring the needle up at 1, insert at 2, and then bring the needle back up at 3 (Figure 1). Finish by inserting the needle at 4 (Figure 2). Repeat for the desired number of stitches.

FIGURE 1   FIGURE 2

Detached Chain Stitch

Working from top to bottom, bring the needle up at 1 and reinsert at 1 to create a loop; do not pull the thread taut. Bring the needle up at 2, through the loop, and gently pull the needle toward you to pull the loop flush with the fabric (Figure 1). Insert the needle at 3 to finish the stitch (Figures 2 and 3).

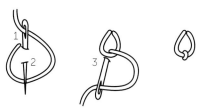

FIGURE 1   FIGURE 2   FIGURE 3

Feather Stitch

Working from top to bottom, bring the needle up at 1, reinsert at 2, and bring back up at 3, looping the thread under the needle (Figure 1). Insert the needle at 4 and bring it up at 5, looping the thread under the needle (Figure 2). Repeat for the desired number of stitches (Figure 3).

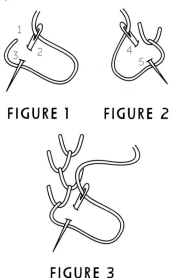

FIGURE 1   FIGURE 2

FIGURE 3

Fly Stitch

Working from top to bottom, bring the needle up at 1, reinsert at 2, and bring up at 3, catching the thread under the needle and pulling taut (*Figure 1*). Insert the needle at 4 and bring up at 5 (*Figure 2*). Repeat for the desired number of stitches (*Figure 3*).

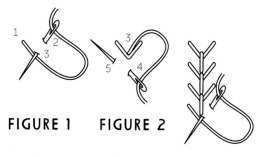

FIGURE 1   FIGURE 2

FIGURE 3

French Knot

Bring the needle up at 1 and hold the thread taut about 2" (5 cm) above the fabric. Point the needle toward your fingers and wrap the thread tautly around the needle twice (*Figure 1*). Insert the needle into the fabric near 1 and complete the knot by holding the thread taut near the wrapped thread as you pull the needle toward the wraps and through the fabric (*Figure 2*).

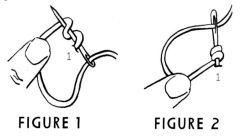

FIGURE 1   FIGURE 2

Herringbone Stitch

Draw two parallel lines on the fabric with tailor's chalk. Bring the needle up at 1 on the lower line, reinsert at 2 on the upper line, and bring up at 3 (*Figure 1*). Insert the needle at 4 on the lower line and bring up at 1 (*Figure 2*). Repeat for the desired number of stitches (*Figure 3*).

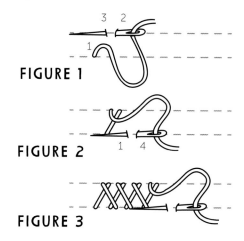

FIGURE 1

FIGURE 2

FIGURE 3

Lazy Daisy Stitch

Working from top to bottom, bring the needle up at 1 and create a loop by reinserting at 1; do not pull the thread taut. Bring the needle back up at 2, keeping the needle above the loop and pulling the needle toward you gently to tighten the loop so that it is flush with the fabric (*Figure 1*). Tack the loop down by inserting the needle at 3 (*Figure 2*). Repeat for the desired number of stitches.

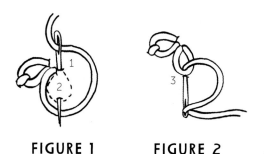

FIGURE 1   FIGURE 2

Ribbon Rose

With embroidery thread, stitch a five-pointed "star" *(Figure 1)*. Thread a larger needle with ribbon and bring up the needle at the center of the star. Weave the needle under and over the legs of the star in a spiral *(Figure 2)* until the shape has been filled *(Figure 3)*.

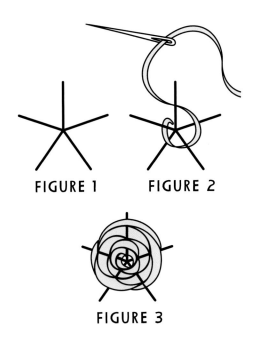

FIGURE 1   **FIGURE 2**

FIGURE 3

Satin Stitch

Generally worked from left to right, satin stitch is most often used to fill in a shape or create a thick, scallop-like edge. Bring the needle up at 1, insert at 2, and bring back up at 3. Repeat.

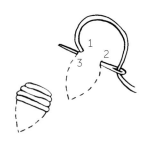

Seed Stitch

Small straight stitches worked in clusters or scattered at random. Seed stitches can also be worked tightly together and all in the same direction to uniformly fill a space.

Stem Stitch

Working from left to right, bring the needle up at 1 and insert the needle ⅛–¼" (3–6 mm) away at 2. Bring the needle up halfway between 1 and 2, at 3 *(Figure 1)*. Keeping the newly created loop below the needle and stitchline, pull the stitch taut. Continue by inserting the needle ⅛–¼" (3–6 mm) to the right of 2, then bring up the needle to the right of 2 *(Figure 2)*.

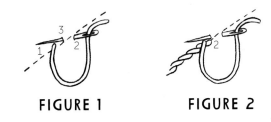

FIGURE 1   **FIGURE 2**

Straight/Running Stitch

Working from left to right, bring the needle up and insert at 1, ⅛–¼" (3–6 mm)" from the starting point. Bring the needle up at 2 (⅛–¼" [3–6 mm] to the left of 1) and repeat.

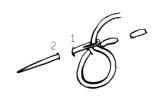

Index

acrylic paint 18
alphabet 129
appliqué 74–81

backstitch 138
batiks 17
batting 30–31
bias, fabric 136
bindings 132–134
blanket stitch 138
borders, sewing 132
brushes 29

chain stitch 138; detached 139
chevron stitch 138
collage, fabric 100–101, 108–109
color, choosing 34–35
color pigments 23
cotton 17
couching stitch 139
crayons, fabric 21
cross-stitch 139
cutter and mat 30

decorative stitches 25
doodles, machine 56–57
dyeing fabric 17, 22
Dye-Na-Flow 21
dyes, fabric 21

embroidery hoop 32
embroidery stitches 25

fabric, hand-dyed 17
fabric paint 18–21

fabric preparation for coloring 19
fabrics 15–17
feather stitch 139
felt, wool 17
fiberfill 30
finishing knot 136
floss, embroidery 23
fly stitch 140
free-motion sewing 42
freezer paper 32
French knot 140

grain, fabric 136

handstitching 62–63
herringbone stitch 140

ink, fabric 21, 32
interfacing, fusible 30, 33
iron 33

knots 135–136

lazy daisy stitch 140
lightbox 28

machine, sewing 30, 33
markers, fabric 21
metallic thread 25
mixed-media art fabric 94–95
muslin 15

needlefelting 114–115
needles 30

painting fabric 22, 40–41
paints 18–19
pearl cotton thread 25
pencils, fabric 21
pins 33
prepared for dyeing (PDF) fabric 17

quilter's knot 135

ribbon rose 141
running stitch 141

satin stitch 141
scissors 32
seam allowance 136
seed stitch 141
selvedge 136
silk thread 25
sleeve, hanging 135
slip stitch 137
square knot 136
squaring up fabric 132
stem stitch 141
stencils 29, 68–69
straight stitch 141
supplies and tools 28–30

textile mediums 20
threads 23–25
topstitching 137
transfers, image 122

whipstitch 137
workspace 15

Acknowledgments

With much love and appreciation to my husband, Tom, and children, Meghan, Matthew, Kevin, and Brian, for always encouraging my vision and supporting my "squirrel and shiny things" thoughts. I'm also grateful to each of them for tolerating my creative chaos in the two converted bedroom studios and creative art crumbs that end up all over the house.

To Jeanne Cook-Delpit, my BERNINA mentor, whose unbridled energy, fireball passion, and enthusiasm for my art and mission inspire endless possibilities in my creative sewing journey every day.

This wouldn't be a sewing- and stitching-themed book without the role models I had growing up. I watched my Grandma Zawacki, Grandma Jaskolski, and Aunt Ann Boucher magically transform fabric, threads, and fibers into masterpieces of art that have withstood the test of time.

Resources

THREADS
Aurifil (aurifil.com)
Floriani Thread (mkdistributing.com)
Isacord Thread (isacordthread.com)
Sue Spargo Thread Collection (suespargo.com)
Valdani, Inc. (valdani.com)
Weeks Dye Works (weeksdyeworks.com)
WonderFil Specialty Threads (wonderfilonline.com)

SEWING MACHINES
BERNINA of America (bernina.com)

FABRIC PAINTS AND DYES
DecoArt (decoart.com)
I Love To Create/Tulip Brand (ilovetocreate.com)
Jacquard (jacquardproducts.com)

NEEDLES
John James (jjneedles.com)
Piecemakers (piecemakers.com)
Schmetz Needles (schmetzneedles.com)

FUSIBLE WEB AND BATTING
Mistyfuse (mistyfuse.com)
Pellon (pellonprojects.com)
Quilter's Select (quiltersselect.com)
Warm and Natural (warmcompany.com)

SCISSORS
Havel's Scissors (havelssewing.com)
Karen Kay Buckley Scissors (karenkaybuckley.com)

ART SUPPLIES
Caran d'Ache (carandache.com)
ColourArte (colourarte.com)
Derwent (pencils.co.uk)
Golden (goldenpaints.com)
Liquitex (liquitex.com)
Sakura (sakuraofamerica.com)
Stencil Girl (stencilgirlproducts.com)
Tombow (tombowusa.com)

INSPIRATION AND ONLINE INSTRUCTION
Craft Daily (craftdaily.com)
Quilting Arts TV (quiltingdaily.com)
The Quilt Show (thequiltshow.com)

fw
a content + ecommerce company

www.fwmedia.com

20 19 18 17 16   5 4 3 2 1

Distributed in Canada by Fraser Direct
100 Armstrong Avenue
Georgetown, ON, Canada L7G 5S4
Tel: (905) 877-4411

Distributed in the U.K. and Europe by
F&W MEDIA INTERNATIONAL
Brunel House, Newton Abbot, Devon,
TQ12 4PU, England
Tel: (+44) 1626 323200,
Fax: (+44) 1626 323319
Email: enquiries@fwmedia.com

Distributed in Australia by Capricorn Link
P.O. Box 704, S. Windsor NSW,
2756 Australia
Tel: (02) 4560 1600 Fax: (02) 4577 5288
Email: books@capricornlink.com.au

SRN: 16MM01
ISBN-13: 978-1-63250-205-6

Editor Michelle Bredeson
Designer Bekah Thrasher
Production Coordinator Bryan Davidson
Beauty Photographer Donald Scott
Stylist Ann Sabin Swanson
Flat Photographer Tony Jacobsen
Illustrator Missy Shepler

We make every effort to ensure the accuracy of our instructions, but mistakes occasionally occur. Errata can be found at quiltingdaily.com/errata.

Let Your **CREATIVITY SHINE** with These Resources from Interweave